WINNING
IT BACK

GARY WILTSHIRE

WINNING
IT BACK

RACING POST

This edition first published in Great Britain in 2011 by
Racing Post Books
Raceform, High Street, Compton, Newbury, Berkshire, RG20 6NL

1 3 5 7 9 10 8 6 4 2

A catalogue record for this book is available from the British Library.

ISBN 978-1-905156-82-5

Designed by Soapbox
www.soapbox.co.uk

Printed and bound in Great Britain by the MPG Books Group

Every effort has been made to fulfil requirements with regard to copyright material. The author and publisher will be glad to rectify any omissions at the earliest opportunity.

www.racingpost.com/shop

The photos in the book are from the author's collection, with the following exceptions: Bentico: Kenneth Bright; Suivez: David Hastings; Sotheby's sale: Frank Baron; Mi Odds at Hereford: Pleasure Prints; Gary with Norma Macauley: Les Hurley; with Dave Smith: Steve Nash/Racing Post; with John Parrott: Colin Turner; outside Sotherbys: Frank Baron/Guardian News & Media Ltd.

Contents

'The "Magnificent Seven" at Ascot in September 1996 was the greatest day of my racing life – and the worst day of Gary Wiltshire's. How he came back was almost as amazing as how he got there in the first place. Read his story.'

FRANKIE DETTORI

'They don't come any larger than life than Gary Wiltshire. Beneath that big smile lies a brilliant brain and an extraordinary story.'

JOHN PARROTT

First off ...

Now that you've got over the shock of discovering that 'The Belly from the Telly' has written a book, allow me to mention the two people who, more than any others, have made *Winning It Back* possible:

Frankie Dettori, without whose 'Magnificent Seven' at Ascot in September 1996 nobody would ever have heard of Gary Wiltshire. Talk about every cloud having a silver lining.

And my wife Sue, who has had to put up with living with a compulsive gambler for all these years. Not being a punter herself, she's somehow managed to keep me on the straight and narrow. Thanks for everything, babe!

I hope you enjoy reading this as much as I enjoyed writing it.

Be lucky

Gary Wiltshire

An open goal

A bell was clanging. It was sounding for my funeral. At Ascot racecourse they still ring a bell as the runners enter the home straight – it's one of the many quaint old traditions which the course keeps going. Another is the age-old tradition of some poor sod doing his bollocks in the betting ring. This time round that poor sod was me.

The Ascot bell was ringing to announce the climax of the seventh and last race on Saturday 28 September 1996, which for ever after would be known as Dettori Day.

The charismatic Italian jockey had won the first six races on that afternoon's programme. Winning the seventh would make racing history, but his final ride that day, a horse named Fujiyama Crest, did not look to have much of a chance of playing his part.

The horse's form was not good enough for him to win the race. Simple as that – and an open goal for that amply uphol-stered bookie betting at the lower end of the rails, with his little sign reading: 'GARY WILTSHIRE'.

An avalanche of money had pushed down Fujiyama Crest's odds for the race down to around 2-1, an insane price for a horse who had been widely available at as long as 20-1 that morning.

For a bookmaker faced with such a position, there was only one thing to do – and I did it, laying Fujiyama Crest for ever-increasing sums of money to other bookmakers who were looking to lessen their own liabilities as the avalanche continued.

The only thing that could go wrong was that Fujiyama Crest would win, but that remote possibility didn't figure in my thinking.

It was as if my whole life as a gambler had led to those few chaotic minutes . . .

1

'I was a cheeky bastard,
even in those days'

G̲ambling is in my blood. Go as far back in my family as you like, and you'll find that most of us have always liked a little bet – though not many of my predecessors ever let gambling dominate their lives in quite the way that I have.

From my earliest days, betting was all around me, a part of my life.

My Dad's dad Jack Wiltshire had the best flower stall in Leather Lane, one of London's most popular street markets, and he used to go racing every Monday. In those days, before high-street betting shops opened in 1961, the racecourse was the only legal place to have a bet, unless you had a credit account. Jack loved a punt, so regular as clockwork every Monday he'd dress up smart and take the bus up to 'Ally Pally' – the now defunct Alexandra Park at the foot of Muswell Hill in north London, where meetings were often held in the evenings – or catch the train to Brighton or Lewes on the south coast, courses which while a fair way from the capital were part of the London-based racing fan's usual beat.

(The more upmarket courses near London like Sandown or Kempton Park – not to mention the poshest of the lot, Ascot – rarely raced on a Monday, and Monday was Jack's day off.)

Jack died before I was born, so I was never able to sit on his knee and hear him reminisce about his biggest winners – all punters want to tell you about their winners and conveniently leave out all the losers, don't they? – but before I came along he was certainly the big racing man in the family.

The big racing lady was on my mother's side of my pedigree. My grandmother Alice Truscott used to have a punt every day – just half a crown or so, but it was one of her greatest pleasures. She didn't bother with form and weights and all that sort of thing, but went through the race programmes in the paper each morning and picked her selections from their names. She especially liked horses with simple human names: Tom, Dick and Harry would have made a nice treble for Alice!

She lived in a fifth-floor council flat on Ironmonger Row in Islington, on the edge of central London, where I'd be a frequent visitor. Once I'd started to get interested in betting, she was always telling me, 'You'll own a betting shop one day, Gal' – 'Gal' was always what my family called me – 'and I'll come and be your cleaner.' I did get to own a betting shop – at Raunds, near Kettering in Northamptonshire – but dear old Alice didn't live long enough to be employed as the cleaner.

My parents Eddie and Pat Wiltshire enjoyed – and still enjoy – a modest punt, but to be honest they weren't very good at betting. Like Alice, Dad tended to select dogs or horses whose names took his fancy, while Mum's favourite bets on the dogs were combination forecasts of traps 1, 2 and 4 – and any punter on the greyhounds leaves out traps 5 and 6 at their peril.

After gambling, the other great theme of my life has been food, and an enthusiasm for scoff must also be in my blood. During the war Dad had served in the Army at Aldershot, and guess what: he worked in the catering department of the NAAFI.

Mum and Dad had married very young. They always told me that I'd been conceived in Southend-on-Sea – I never asked for more details – but when I was born, at five minutes after midnight on 5 December 1954, they were living in Lever Street, Islington.

The family home was a flat over their shop, where they sold cheap household goods – pots, pans, brushes, mops, that sort of thing. Next door was a pub called the Wellington, and directly across the road a betting shop named Harry Barham opened in 1961, when I was six. Even at that age I'd stare out the window at the sign and wonder what mysterious goings-on took place in there, and perhaps I should have taken heed of what happened to Harry and steered well clear of the world of betting: I can't remember why or how, but he was murdered.

When I was very young Mum and Dad took me in my pram to Harringay dogs, and I loved it. So what chance did I have of not turning out a gambler? Dog racing, even more than the horses, was my first love, and as long ago as I can remember I was thrilled by the speed and the grace of greyhounds. More than anything at that stage of my life, it was my dream to own and race a greyhound.

When I was four I started making up my private games around betting. I had a set of playing cards, from which I made

17

my own dog race game, which I imagined taking place at King's Heath, the Birmingham dog track where I knew they raced every Saturday evening as I'd seen the name in the paper. (It's odd to think that I'm writing these words at home in Hollywood, on the edge of Birmingham, and King's Heath is not far away.)

Having removed the four kings from the pack of cards, I'd arrange them at the head of four lanes, shuffle the remaining pack and then take out a card. If it was a heart, I'd move the King of Hearts one place forward, then I'd take another card from the pack and move whichever King matched that suit – and so on until one of the Kings reached the finish line. I'd have imaginary bets on the outcome, and was absorbed by this for hour after hour.

When I was five years old I went to my first horse race. Mum and Dad had a caravan at Combe Haven, near Hastings, and one year they took me to the Romney Marsh point-to-point, which was held at a place with the wonderfully rural name of Lamb Farm, East Guldeford. Even now I can remember the excitement of the racecourse: the atmosphere, the noise, the colour, the amazingly brave jockeys, and most of all the magnificent horses with such strange and sometimes exotic names. The first winner was ridden by Bob Hacking on a horse called Peter Rock – and then the same jockey won the second race on Black Jean and the third on Young Teal.

The fourth race was the Ladies' Race, which put paid to the Romney Marsh point-to-point 1960 being an uncanny forerunner of a certain jockey going through the card thirty-six years later, with big consequences for Yours Truly.

Dad was interested in all sorts of sports. He used to take me to watch the boxing at Shoreditch Town Hall or the Majestic in Finsbury Park, and in those days my great sporting heroes were Vic Andretti, the local champion from Hoxton, and the heavyweight Billy Walker. Nowadays Billy is more remembered than Vic. Known as 'The Blond Bomber', he'd been – among other things – a porter in Billingsgate Fish Market before becoming a professional boxer, and under the management of his brother George he went to the top, or at least very close to the top.

I was mad keen on boxing for much of my childhood, and remember one Christmas waking up and going downstairs to get my presents from under the tree. There was a beautiful dressing gown like boxers wore as they came into the ring – in my size and with the name 'GARY WILTSHIRE' embroidered on the back!

Not only because I had the dressing gown which so made me look the part, I started trying my hand at boxing at the Lyon Club in Hoxton, but after a while I had to give up. My Dad said it was because I was getting too many nose-bleeds, but I knew that it was because I was simply not good enough.

Sport also played an important part in our Saturday trips to Southend.

I (and later my sister Jackie, who was born ten years after me, almost to the very day) would clamber into Dad's Dormobile – KYN422D: funny how you never forget car registration numbers

– and off we'd go down the Arterial Road. It was like a mini-holiday every weekend, the great Londoners' day out.

As soon as we arrived in Southend we'd have an ice cream from Rossi's, near the pier, before tucking in to a huge plate of fish and chips at a place called Bailey's.

Southend was every Cockney's dream resort. Everyone in our area wanted to move out there, and until we could do that, going every weekend was the next best thing. Our family loved the Shoeburyness end of the sea front rather than the Westcliff-on-Sea end. My Dad used to say that the Westcliff-on-Sea end was too posh for the likes of us, but eventually I twigged that he preferred the Shoeburyness end because the parking was cheaper down there! So we'd park there, then walk to the pier and get on the little train which took you right out to the end of the pier. Magic!

We'd go to Southend dog track – where later I'd work the market which was held in the centre of the track, selling bulbs – and if my parents had won a few quid we'd stay over so that we could spend some of Sunday in the bracing sea air as well.

What with the dogs and the point-to-points, I was now getting exposed to betting big time, and the more I experienced the atmosphere it created, the more fascinated by it I became.

I loved watching the racing on the television, especially in the days of the old ITV Seven, when the racing on that channel every Saturday was seven races, and the challenge was to pick the winners of all of them in a seven-leg accumulator. The ITV Seven was part of the weekend in so many households in those days, though understandably it was not often won.

All this had a deep effect on me. From the age of five or six I knew how betting worked, and could calculate the returns. Working with the odds always came naturally – like the bookie's kid who starts at infant school, and tells the teacher that he can count, and when she asks him to do so, goes: 'Evens, 11-10, 6-5, 11-8, 6-4, 13-8 …'.

And when I outgrew the King's Heath card game which I'd invented, I spent years playing with *Escalado*, that brilliant horse racing game which, unlike board games, had a sort of feel for the real thing.

Escalado, which dated back to the 1920s, consisted of a long and narrow green fabric which you stretched across the dining room table. At the starting end of the race the fabric was attached to the table with some brackets and rubber bands, while at the finishing end there was a small box which you clamped to the table, and coming out of this box was a handle.

There were five horses, coloured white (though real horses are always called grey, not white), yellow, red, blue and green, and back then they were made of lead – before we knew all about lead poisoning. You'd line the horses up at the start, and then furiously turn the handle in the box, which caused the fabric to vibrate and the horses to move forward. Just to complicate matters, along the course there were three 'fences' in the form of little puck-shaped cylinders of wood, placed across the course but leaving gaps just wide enough for the horses to get through. The knack was to get your horse past these obstacles without losing ground by bashing into them.

It was fantastic fun and must have been a first taste of the potential excitement of racing for loads of kids like me, though the particular influence of *Escalado* on my young brain was that it gave me lots of practice in how to make a book. For every race I ran, I'd call out imaginary odds about each horse, and I always wanted to have the white horse on my side, as I've always loved greys – in *Escalado* as in real life. The set included toy money – a bit like *Monopoly* money – and each time I played I learned more and more about how a book works and what it means in terms of the actual cash.

(The modern *Escalado* is more sophisticated in some ways, though as it's a Flat racing version – complete with starting stalls – there is less potential for mayhem than my 'steeplechasing' version had. And now the horses are made of plastic and have detachable plastic jockeys – so if you name one of your jockeys Lester Piggott, he can jock off another jockey in order to get the best chance.)

As soon as I was old enough I started helping my parents out at the Leather Lane flower stall, which was only open between noon and 2pm, Monday to Friday: it catered for all the offices round that area, so there was no point in opening at other times.

Working there was fantastic fun: all that banter among the traders, the laughs with the customers, the hustle and bustle and learning how to make a few quid through your own wits.

One of the most frequent customers at our stall was a lady named Violet Kray, whose twin sons Reggie and Ronnie were – how shall I put this? – very influential in the local community. Mrs Kray was a keen gardener and regularly came to buy flowers and bulbs, occasionally accompanied by one or both of her sons – diamond geezers, or so they seemed to me at the time.

My first school was Goswell Road Primary School, but as far as I was concerned it could equally have been named Pentonville Prison. Not only was it so grim that it looked and felt like a jail, but they locked the gates at 9am to stop anyone escaping, and didn't open them again until going-home time at 3.30. This being locked in drove me up the wall, because – as you'll shortly find out – throughout my school days I liked to take a little stroll outside during my lunch hour.

And another thing. The school seemed to have been plonked in a sea of tarmac or concrete. There wasn't a blade of grass to be seen. Come to think of it, for most of my childhood I never got to see grass. Every now and again we'd get over to Lincoln's Inn Fields, which was lovely, but not exactly huge swathes of lawn – and that was it. Perhaps that's why I've always loved getting out into the country – though I'll always be a Londoner at heart – and surrounding myself with all that lovely grass and fresh air at a racecourse or point-to-point.

From Goswell Road Primary School I'd gone on to Barnsbury, where even though I hadn't yet reached my teenage years, it didn't take me long to become the class bookmaker. In this role I won a few quid, but it's the losses you privately recall more keenly, and I'll never forget the 1966 Derby.

In those days the Derby was run on a Wednesday, and there was much more build-up in the non-racing press than there is now, so that even boys with no interest in racing at all were keen to make a few shillings by having a bet.

I was already well versed in studying the form, and over the few days before the race I spent most of my time with my nose in the *Sporting Life*. One thing was apparent: the hotly fancied Charlottown, trained by Gordon Smyth and ridden by 52-year-old Scobie Breasley, wouldn't win. He'd been unbeaten in three races as a two-year-old, but in his only outing before the Derby couldn't do better than finish runner-up to a less than top class animal named Black Prince II in the Derby Trial at Lingfield Park. Worse, as far as his Derby prospects were concerned, Charlottown had stuck his head in the air when coming under pressure and did not appear to be enjoying himself one bit – far from ideal behaviour in a potential Derby horse.

So when my classmates came and gathered round me to get a little financial interest in the biggest Flat race of the season, I was firmly of the opinion that I could lay Charlottown until the cows came home. I laid him to a good few bets of ten shillings – fifty pence in this new-fangled decimal currency we have now – though most of the lads were more tentative and opted for my minimum stake of four shillings (twenty pence).

The race was due off at 3.30, but the start was delayed a quarter of an hour. Charlottown (led up at Epsom by Michael Jarvis, who went on to become a top trainer before announcing his retirement early in 2011) had lost a shoe while walking round the paddock – that old Epsom parade ring, which was about two miles' walk from the stands – and had to be reshod.

I'd managed to sneak away from school before the last lesson of the day began, and found a handy little television shop nearby where I could watch the race on one of the tellies – black and white in those days, of course – displayed in the window. That delay increased my chances of being nabbed by a teacher or prefect making a quick getaway from school, but no one came along – so I was able to watch in horror as Scobie brought Charlottown with a characteristic sweetly timed run up the rail to collar the leader Pretendre, ridden by Paul Cook, very close home and win by a neck.

Just as on a much more significant losing day thirty years later, I faced financial ruin. And just as with that later occasion, I told myself that the only way out was to pay up like a man – or like a boy in 1966 – and work my fingers to the bone wheeling and dealing until the whole debt was cleared.

The following week I skived off school, managed to appropriate a few trays of peaches from the Dormobile when Mum and Dad's attention was elsewhere, and went house to house trying to raise a few quid to pay off the debts.

Most of my classmates were happy to wait for payment – well, they could hardly go and complain to the form teacher, could they? – and within about two weeks I was solvent again.

After I'd been at Barnsbury a while the school amalgamated with Highbury Grove, the all-boys comprehensive where the headmaster was the famous – some might say notorious – Dr Rhodes Boyson, later a Tory MP and back then famous for his mutton-chop whiskers and for his distinct views about education, especially school discipline.

One of his convictions – as I was soon to find out – was that corporal punishment was a perfectly reasonable deterrent to bad behaviour.

Trouble was, he and I had different views about what constituted bad behaviour, but I suppose that had I given the matter some thought, I'd have guessed that Boyson would have taken a dim view of his pupils being caught hanging around a betting shop during the lunch hour.

Racing in Britain had been completely transformed when the first high-street betting shops opened in May 1961, when I was six, and as I grew older they exerted an ever more magnetic appeal – especially when I should have been concentrating on school work.

As the bell went for lunchtime at Highbury Grove I'd hook up with a couple of mates and we'd sneak out the school back gate and down to the nearest bookies' shop. We were under age and knew that we wouldn't be served had we tried to place bets inside, so we waited until a punter with a suitably kind face came along and asked him or her to put the bets on for us.

In those days there was only a very bare commentary on the races – no pictures – and we'd hang around outside, catching what we could of the action. If we won, the kindly go-between would bring our winnings out to us.

The trouble was, of course, that when hanging around outside the shop we'd easily be seen by passers-by – and sure enough, one fateful day one of the Highbury Grove teachers caught us loitering with intent. Back we were marched to school and straight into the headmaster's study – with the result that the following morning we were paraded in front of school assembly, made to line up, hold out our non-writing hand, wait for Boyson to raise his long cane, then THWACK! THWACK! THWACK! for as many times as he fancied.

Ever the bright spark, it quickly dawned on me that if you relaxed your fingers slightly and made a shallow cup of your hand just before the cane was brought down, rather than keep your hand rigid, the pain would be a good deal less. So I survived without permanent physical or mental damage.

School work was never my strong point. I could work out an each-way treble just like that, but if somebody asked me how to calculate the relationship between the radius and the circumference of a circle, that was a lost world to me. I thought a circle was what dogs ran round in!

By the time I was a teenager, greyhounds and horses had been joined by a real passion for football, and that too was in my blood. A more than useful goalkeeper, my Dad had had a trial for Arsenal, whose famous Highbury Stadium was not far from where we lived. The Gunners did not in the end sign him up, but he went on to play for Brentford.

When I was very small Dad used to take me on Sunday mornings to the Hare and Hounds pub on the Leyton Road, behind which was a football pitch which every week had a game between two of the best local teams. They must have been pretty good, as you had to pay to get in.

A side activity while watching these games at the Hare and Hounds was betting. A couple of bookmakers were always there

– I remember that one of them was called One-Arm Lou (for the obvious reason), whom later on I'd often see at Walthamstow dog track – and knowing which team my Dad had backed added an extra dimension to the excitement.

So did stopping on the way home at the Jewish bakery in Green Lanes, where we bought delicious bagels and cakes – remember, other shops weren't open on Sundays then, so stocking up at Grozinsky's added to the fun.

You might find this hard to believe, given that not long ago I went over the 32 stone mark and had put my name to a newspaper column which called me 'The Belly from the Telly', but when I was a kid I was not only properly proportioned, I was also pretty agile and athletic, which made it natural for me to follow the family tradition of playing in goal.

I'd played a bit at Goswell Road School, but it was when I was at Highbury Grove that my goalkeeping talent started to get noticed. I played for the school team, and showed sufficient talent to be called up to play for Islington Schoolboys, and in due course for London Schoolboys. I was even summoned to Brisbane Road to have a trial for Leyton Orient, but sadly nothing came of that.

Islington Schoolboys was a team selected from all the schools in the borough and managed by John Drabwell, one of the pair of twins who at the time were famous in non-league football. They were closely involved with Walthamstow Avenue, the club that back then was to amateur football what Real Madrid was to the professional game.

The great footballing nursery in the area was Holloway School, where the coach there was none other than the legendary Arsenal goalie Bob Wilson. For years the school had been providing a steady stream of players into the Highbury first team – including the great Charlie George, who was four years older than me and my real hero.

In fact there was an almost blanket domination by Holloway School, not only as a feeder for the Gunners but also for Islington. Boys from there could be very hostile to anyone else, and in the dressing room or on the bus to the training ground they simply wouldn't pay me the slightest attention.

After a while I got used to this and just kept myself to myself, but while that sort of ill feeling off the field was very aggravating, on the field it badly ate away at team spirit.

Matters came to a head one day when we were playing one of the East End borough teams. Before we got on the bus to the match, John Drabwell took me on one side, saying he wanted a quiet word. He pointed out that for that game Holloway School was fielding ten of the eleven players in the side; the eleventh was the goalie G. Wiltshire. But the reserve keeper was from Holloway, John said, and he'd become aware that the other lads had been cooking up a scheme to get me out the way and have their schoolmate replace me. I should be on my guard during the match.

I brushed this aside and cockily insisted that I could look after myself, but I should have paid more attention to what he'd said.

When early in the game a high ball came into my penalty area I was running out to collect it, calling out 'My ball!', when our centre-half deliberately got there before me and headed the ball into the net. Own goal!

I was livid, and could have murdered that tosser. I leapt on his back and started pummelling him, which of course the referee saw in an instant, and I was dismissed from the field. The Holloway boys had set a trap for me and I'd walked straight into it. Their keeper would be taking over for Islington Boys in the future.

Being sent off left me a disgraced player and a marked man as far as the borough's football authorities were concerned, and I never played for Islington Boys again. To be truthful, that incident cost me a lot of my enthusiasm for football, and before long I gave up playing.

But I still loved the game, and continued as a fervent Arsenal supporter. It would have taken wild horses to keep me from a game at Highbury, and on one occasion not even a broken arm stopped me going.

Before an evening game I'd asked my Dad to drop me off at the stadium, but he said he couldn't, as they were going out. In fact, he said, it would be better if I didn't go to the match at all, as they wouldn't be able to collect me after the game and they didn't want me wandering the streets late at night.

So when they'd gone for the evening I went and got my bike out, and cycled off in the direction of Highbury. It was a few miles away, but I was confident I'd get there without mishap.

Wrong. I was pedalling through Canonbury minding my own business when the front wheel caught something in the road and I fell off. I had a terrible pain in my right arm, but there was no way I was going to miss the match, so I hid the bike behind some bushes and walked the rest of the way.

After the game I walked back – slowly, as my arm was hurting more and more – and found the bike, but by now the arm was so bad that I could barely get onto the saddle, let alone ride it. When after what seemed like hours I managed to get home, Mum and Dad, who'd just got in, saw the state I was in and took me off to the hospital. The arm was broken, and I spent the next few weeks in plaster.

But at least I'd got to see the game.

The best day of all for me as an Arsenal fan was when we won the championship by beating Spurs at White Hart Lane in 1971. Our entire household supported Arsenal, and we had some party that night!

It's a matter of great pride to me that the family footballing tradition has been carried on by my eldest son Nicky, who has showed himself a more than useful goalkeeper. He was offered terms to play for Watford but he declined, as he thought he was more of a centre-forward than a goalie. I was choked that he didn't take his football further, but that's kids for you: you work your bollocks off to make sure they grow up in the right way, and then they just go off and do what they like anyway.

And more recently my youngest son Charlie also showed great promise as a goalie, and has even been coached by the Aston Villa legend Nigel Spink. But he too found being a goalie too restricting. It strikes me as a shame that members of the family from different generations were mad keen football players but none of us made it to the top.

Mum and Dad moved around a fair bit when I was a kid: from Lever Street to a fifteenth-floor flat nearby in King Square, then to Market Place, Holloway. But wherever we were, Leather Lane market in Holborn was my real home, the one place where I just loved to be.

There was an old Italian church close by, but an institution which loomed larger in most of our lives was Harvey and Thompson, the pawn shop, with its mightily imposing front door where you'd go to sell jewellery, and the poky little door down the alley where you'd go if you were pawning something else.

At a time before credit cards had become the standard way of stretching your funds, pawning your valuables was simply a fact of life. If you were short of the readies, for whatever reason, first port of call was the pawnbroker's. Say you needed £50, you might take a ring worth £100 into the pawn shop, and they would lend you the £50 in cash against it. When you were back in funds, you'd go and redeem it, for the £50 plus interest. It was only when that ring had been unredeemed after three months that it would appear for sale in the pawn shop window.

Going to the pawnbroker may have been routine back then, but you might not want your nosy neighbours in Leather Lane market having a gander when you were going through a difficult patch – in which case you'd make a trip out to the pawn shop in the Seven Sisters Road, near Tottenham, where your transactions would be conducted in greater privacy and you were less likely to be copped sneaking in.

Another great institution at Leather Lane market was the sweet stall, run by my Dad's Italian mate Mikey Falco. I loved pinching the coconut macaroons when Mikey wasn't looking, but even better was talking to him about greyhounds and horses and betting. It made me feel like there was a magical world out there, full of glamour and excitement. I couldn't wait to be part of it.

Mikey was like a second father to me, and when years later I told him that I was determined to be a bookie, he never for one moment discouraged me. Other people were saying, 'Why don't you get a proper job, like driving a bus?', but I knew what I wanted and Mikey supported me every inch of the way.

When I was about fourteen, the family moved out to the leafy area just on the edge of London at Enfield, where Mum and Dad for the first time in their lives bought a house: 900 Great Cambridge Road, which cost them £5,000.

I started at Bishop Stopford's School, where my best subjects were Maths and English, but at first it was a lonely time as I didn't know anybody locally, and apart from football had no interests I could easily share with others. Although Enfield was only just outside London, it felt to me like a different country altogether after I'd grown up in the centre of the city, and I felt very isolated.

By now I was even keener on betting, and it was a stroke of luck when I was put in charge of the school greenhouse. Each morning I'd buy the *Sporting Life* on the way to get the bus to school, and couldn't wait for lunchtime, when I'd potter off to do my duties in the greenhouse – a great cover for sitting and absorbing all that the *Life* could tell me about that day's racing. Having made my selections, I'd put a coat on over my school uniform, nip out to the nearest betting shop – 'Brookes of Enfield Wash', it said over the front – and ask someone to have my ten bob or a pound on, then get back in good time for the start of the afternoon's lessons.

On my way home after the end of the school day I'd ditch the *Sporting Life*, so my parents never knew what I was up to.

In those days I sometimes thought the *Life* was my only friend, and I certainly had no interest in girls: I'd get all the romance I wanted from a five-bob Super Yankee, thank you very much.

One of the betting shop punters who regularly put my bets on for me was called Chris Barker, who as well as enjoying a punt loved to own a few greyhounds at Walthamstow.

I liked nothing more than talking to Chris about dog racing, and I'd often go with him to meetings at Walthamstow. One day after I'd won a few bob I decided that it was time to get a dog of my own, so that I could make a start on achieving my ambition to be the world's greatest ever greyhound trainer.

First step was to borrow off Chris the latest issue of the *Greyhound Owner* magazine and see what might be available within my budget of £10 maximum. After half an hour trawling through the Dogs For Sale section, and cursing how little there seemed to be for someone with my limited means, I decided on a blue brindle dog with the rather uninspiring name of Not Good.

Chris contacted the owner and did the deal, and the next thing I knew we were on our way to Hendon Stadium – now defunct – where we'd arranged to meet Not Good's seller in the car park.

Not Good turned out to be a lovely dog and I was delighted with my purchase, but as Chris drove myself and my new friend back to 900 Great Cambridge Road I realised that in all the excitement of buying the dog I'd omitted to make two rather important arrangements.

The first was to get him a kennel, and the second was to tell Mum and Dad about the addition to the family.

The second of those could wait until the morning, but the first was more urgent – so for want of any better idea I made Not Good as comfortable as I could in the garden shed, put down a bowl of water for him, and shut the door.

I expected that he'd be so tired from the palaver of being sold that he'd sleep through until the morning, and I crept into the house and up to bed.

At about half past ten Not Good decided that he'd had enough of being cooped up in the garden shed and started barking to be released – and you can guess easily enough what happened then. Mum and Dad, who liked getting to bed at a sensible hour as they had to get up so early, were awakened by the din and within a couple of minutes were interrogating me about why there was a dog in the shed, with the result that – no ifs and no buts – the following morning Not Good was evicted from the family home.

With my own tail between my legs – never mind Not Good's – I took my precious new acquisition back to Chris, who soon found a good home for him.

After we'd been in Enfield a while I got very pally with a large family called Everest. The sons Wilf, Bob and Gordon were at my school and shared my enjoyment of gambling – Gordon went on to be manager of that Brookes betting shop in Enfield Wash – and every weekend we'd go down to the local working men's club in Ordnance Road to play snooker, cards, darts or bingo, with a good deal of betting on the side to spice things up. It was only then that I started to feel at home in my new life.

So at home, in fact, that I started to make more friends at school, and one day dreamed up a wheeze which I thought would help finance my betting.

Mum and Dad had a long working day. Very early in the morning they'd drive the Dormobile to Cuffley to fill up with flowers at the nursery, then go into the centre of London to Leather Lane market, then back home to Enfield in the evening.

But while the cat's away the mice will play. Some lunchtimes when my presence in the school greenhouse was not urgently required I'd take a group of mates back to our empty house, where I'd cook up and sell them – at two bob a pop – wonderful juicy bacon sandwiches, far more generously filled than you could get in any local caff and liberally coated with tomato ketchup.

I aimed to make a profit of at least two quid a day at this enterprise, and on the way back to school I'd stop off at Brookes of Enfield Wash and get someone to put on my bets for me.

While I spent a great deal of time studying the form, like most punters I had my favourite jockeys, owners and trainers, and in particular I loved the colours of one of the biggest owners of the time, Jim Joel, who was one of the very few owners in history to have won both the Derby (with Royal Palace in 1967) and Grand National (with Maori Venture in 1987). Joel's colours were a very simple black with a red cap, and many years later I started owning racehorses myself – sadly nothing remotely of the quality that Jim Joel had – I got as close as I could to matching those colours. I registered mine as black with navy blue epaulets and armlets with a red cap – which other than close up looked exactly the same as Joel's. (David Wintle, who has trained several horses for me over the years, advised that I should go for dark colours, as they made it harder for the stewards to see what was going on!)

For our summer holidays we sometimes went all the way up to Blackpool, where when I was nine I won the Junior Tarzan competition at the Butlin's holiday camp at the Ocean Hotel. This was less of an achievement than it might sound as I was the only entrant. (And I'm not sure that I'd be the jolly old favourite for the Senior category nowadays.)

I also entered the Best Dressed Boy competition, which, dressed as I was in a lovely made-to-measure suit tailored for me by Toby Norman of Wood Green, I was pretty confident of winning. But I was beaten by some local kid whose clothes looked as if they'd come from Woolworth's, which just goes to show that you're always up against it when playing away.

But in my mid-teens we'd usually go to the caravan at Combe Haven, which for me had the additional attraction of a gilt-edged betting opportunity.

I'd realised very early on in my punting career that decent inside information is the life blood of successful betting, and at Combe Haven I was able to put this theory to profitable practical use in the weekly Donkey Derby, one of the most popular entertainments down there.

Eight donkeys would be brought in by van from Romney Marsh, and the holidaymakers would pay to ride them. Each heat had a field of four donkeys, and at the end of the day the winning riders of the eight heats came together for the two finals.

To add spice to the occasion, there was a ten-shilling Tote, which was very enthusiastically patronised by the crowd.

For most of the holidaymakers these donkey race afternoons were just fantastic fun, but for me they were something much more.

As I was down there for weeks on end, I was able to take a close look at the races, and it didn't take me long to cotton on that only two of the donkeys ever won – the other six were just making up the numbers. This pair of decent donkeys never took each other on in the heats, and only one of the pair would compete in either final.

Mum and Dad always brought down to Combe Haven a massive box of fruit and veg, a fair proportion of which I'd slip to Robin, the bloke who drove the donkey van, and in return he'd tip me the wink if one or other of the good donkeys was below par that day. I was a cheeky bastard, even in those days.

But as I was to learn often enough in later life, even a certainty can be brought down if the jockey isn't up to scratch, and I'd make sure that the rider was good enough before lumping on at the Tote. Of course, anyone could ride these donkeys, but those riders who looked trimmer than the others – or better, who looked as if they knew what they were doing when mounted – were obviously the ones to follow.

So I'd spend time studying the riders, and just to make sure would sidle up and ask casually, 'Are you a horse rider, then?' And if the answer was yes, that was the time to go in big.

I'd regularly clear a decent profit – lovely wonga for a young lad just down for his holidays!

Back home, the dog track nearest Enfield was at Rye House, near Hoddesdon, but it was too small an affair for my liking, and whenever I could I'd catch the Green Line bus and go into town. London was the place for I loved, and win or lose, a night at Harringay or Walthamstow dogs was what I most craved in life.

I'd only bet with stakes of two or three quid, and as in betting shops, as a kid I couldn't legally have a wager with bookmakers on the track, so I'd asked other people to put the bet on for me. They almost always obliged.

It was going to the track – the lights, the crowd, the atmosphere, even the smell – which was so exciting. I loved being there, being involved, just being part of the whole show, and the excitement was the same on each and every visit.

Despite the bacon sandwich business doing so well, I was desperate to leave school as soon as I could, and at sixteen struck out into the big bad world.

I had what felt like a million jobs.

I worked as a van boy for R. White's lemonade, probably best known for the television ad of the bloke raiding the fridge in the middle of the night – with the song confessing that 'I'm a secret lemonade drinker'. This involved turning up at the depot first thing in the morning, loading the van with crates of lemonade, and doing the rounds to help the driver as he delivered to various shops and pubs.

I worked in a wood yard in Edmonton, in an Unwins off-licence, and at Smithfield meat market in London. At Smithfield I wore bumaree overalls – apparently 'bumaree' derives from porters at Billingsgate fish market who used to work on the small ferries known as 'bumboats' – which had very large pockets, and sometimes, when I was loading the van, a dozen lovely juicy sirloin steaks would accidentally find their way into my overalls. No wonder I started to put on a few pounds round the belly.

But deep down all I ever wanted to be was a bookie.

That wouldn't happen quickly though, and when the chance came to start what looked like a dream job, working as a kennel lad for the greyhound trainer Jim Singleton out at Northaw, near Potters Bar, I leapt at it. (Jim was the brother of Randy Singleton, who trained greyhounds for the royal family. It's not only horse racing which has enjoyed royal approval.)

My job involved looking after the dogs: grooming them, exercising them with long walks through the woods, getting them ready for the track and going with them in the van, which was brilliant. If there was one I really fancied, I'd spend extra time grooming him and getting him fit, in the hope that all the special attention would make him run faster. I was working in the world I loved. What could be better?

I'd been there a short while when one afternoon, as we finished loading the greyhounds into the big yellow van to go off to Harringay, one of the girls who worked for Jim slammed down the door of the van onto my finger. I was lucky that my finger was not sliced off, but bad as that would have been, the accident meant that I could not use that finger for any useful purpose – and I decided to apply myself to something less dangerous. Jim was very generous, giving me six months' pay, and – even more important, to my way of thinking at the time – continued to let me have tips when his dogs were running at Harringay.

All this time I was helping out Mum and Dad on the stall in Leather Lane whenever I could, and I'd go round the houses selling flowers and fruit. For the month before Christmas each year they'd sell crackers and festive wrapping paper rather than flowers, and I'd go from house to house flogging those.

Or I'd sell Christmas paper at ten sheets for fifty pence – the currency had gone decimal in February 1971, when I was sixteen

– and find a doorway in one of the streets near the market from which I'd sell it. All very contrary to the street trading rules, but not once did I have my collar felt by the local police, and on a good day I'd get through twenty reams of paper and make a more than decent profit.

Whenever I found myself in a bad position I'd manage to sell my way out of it. I'd be thinking things were pretty grim and there was no light at the end of the tunnel, and somehow I'd see just a glimmer – the tiniest trace – of light, and I knew that there was a way out. This instinct was to stand me in good stead many years later.

My teenage years were dominated by the urge to sell anything to make a few quid – which in practice meant: anything to fuel my addiction to gambling.

I didn't properly realise it yet, but I was already beginning to slide down a slippery slope.

2

'I done me bollocks again'

On the surface my life didn't seem so bad. Between all the other jobs I was working at the Leather Lane market, where some weeks I could earn as much as £100 – not at all bad money for a day's work back then. I bought myself a little ex-Royal Mail van so I had my own transport, and was still living at home on the Great Cambridge Road in Enfield, so didn't have to fork out for rent every week.

But the addiction to betting was getting deeper and deeper. Everything I earned seemed to be going to the bookies. Every week I'd go up to Covent Garden market at Nine Elms, near Vauxhall Bridge, to buy flowers for the stall from a fellow called Reg Gibbons. Reg ran a company named E4 Sales – among his regular customers had been Buster Edwards of Great Train Robbery fame – and he knew about my gambling habit and did his best to help me out.

So I'd turn up at Reg's place, and he'd greet me with, 'Hallo, Wilkie – how did it go over the weekend, son?' And more often than not I'd have to reply, 'No good, Reg – I done me bollocks again.' And he'd slip me a few quid and let me have a load of flowers on credit, telling me I could pay back the money later, when I'd sold the flowers.

I always did pay Reg back, but this hand-to-mouth exist-ence seemed to be going on and on and on, and I was gambling more and more and more. My parents did their best to stop me throwing away my life gambling, and what did I do? I buggered off from them – the only people who could really help me at the time – and found myself a one-bedroom flat in Winchmore Hill, near Palmers Green.

The flat was tiny, with just about room for a single bed and nothing else. The word 'pokey' would hardly do it justice. Worse, it was damp and the wallpaper was peeling off. Worse still, a scrabbling sound from behind the skirting board in the middle of my first night there made me realise that I was far from alone: though I never actually saw the rats, I knew well enough that they were there. All that for eight quid a week!

But at least I could take stock of my life. I had just turned eighteen, had no proper job, and such money as I did earn I was throwing away on gambling. I had to get what passed for real employment, and what did I end up doing? I started work as a board man in a Hector Macdonald's betting shop.

Nowadays betting shops are nice clean places with all the information – runners, prices, results – displayed on loads of television screens round the shop. Back in the 1970s they were much more seedy. There has always been a large number of people who disapprove of gambling – including a good few who do it anyway – and the early betting shops were deliberately miserable places, in order to prevent the young and innocent being attracted into the evil dens of vice.

And technologically they were primitive compared with what we have today. No live television pictures of the dog or horse racing action were allowed – they didn't come in until 1986 – and the information which is now provided on screens was written up on a large board at one end of the shop, where the board man, armed with felt tip pens of different colours, would constantly be updating the information.

For some people this was a terrible job, as you were under relentless pressure to get everything down and not to make a mistake – and you'd get no end of stick from the punters if you did make a rick.

But I thought I was a terrific board man, because my writing was very clear and I knew the whole betting business well – as I should have done, given how much of my life I'd devoted to it.

For me, the platform I stood on to write up all the prices and results was my stage, and from the beginning of betting on the first race of the afternoon to the result of the last race, I was a performer – I was like a top comedian on stage at the London Palladium.

One of our best customers was the late Bobby Smith, who'd played centre-forward in the great Tottenham Hotspur double-winning side in 1961 and had played for England loads of times. Bobby was one of those old-fashioned centre-forwards, lots of brute strength and little finesse, but he had a serious weakness for a punt, to the point of being a compulsive gambler. He and I used to go to Harringay dogs together whenever we could.

For me, every moment on this earth was for betting. I used to get £7 a day for doing the board and was paid daily – and as soon as I had the money in my hand I'd be off to Harringay to play up the seven quid.

One Saturday during my time at Hector Macdonald's the manager told me that the manager of the company's Arnos Grove branch had suddenly been taken ill, and he was going across to fill in for him. Did I think I could take over running our shop while he was away, with just the cashier Mary to help? I saw this as an unexpected opportunity to show that I was good enough to be a manager full time, and instantly agreed.

You weren't allowed to bet in the shop where you worked, but with the manager away, who was to know?

The greyhound races in the late morning didn't present any problem, and I saw that I could be off to a flyer in the first horse race of the afternoon: the favourite was a 5-2 on chance, and I just couldn't see the jolly getting beaten.

I only had about £6 in my pocket, so I thought if I had a bet of £100 to win £40, then I'd have £46 for a decent night out.

I wrote out a slip for the bet – taking care to disguise my writing on the betting slip so that the manager, when he came back, did not see that I'd been betting in my own shop – and sat back to wait for the favourite to win and for me to pay myself out.

It was the same old story. The jolly old favourite got overturned, and all of a sudden I was not only managing the shop on a busy Saturday afternoon, I was chasing my own losses.

Bet followed bet – I had on way more than any of the customers that day – and they all got beaten. The rule was that the branch manager had to phone head office for the OK to take any bet of £200 or more, but I ignored that.

The end of the afternoon, the time when I would have to cash up and parcel up the day's takings to be collected at 5.30 by two members of the company's security staff, was getting closer and closer, and I realised I was in big trouble. Not only was my career as a betting shop manager about to become the shortest in the history of bookmaking; if they discovered that I'd been betting in our shop I was long odds on to lose my job.

I did a quick sum and realised that I was owing the till something in the region of £3,000.

The clock was ticking towards 5.30 – it felt more like High Noon for me – and instead of cashing up, I was racking my brains trying to work out an escape.

The obvious way out – of having all I owed on one final bet – was fraught with danger, and in any case was ruled out, as the racing was over.

And then a miracle happened.

Over the blower, which I thought was closed down for the afternoon, came the words, 'Going into the traps at Harringay …'. The words were delivered in that familiar deadpan voice, but as far as I was concerned the information was being trumpeted by the Angel Gabriel himself.

One more race – and one final chance of saving myself.

Running in that Harringay contest was a dog named Commutering Kid. He was trained by a man I knew well called Frank Melville, and I was aware that he was a very good dog – much better than his odds of 3-1 suggested. So I had £1,100 on him, and stood at the cashier's desk and prayed.

No kidding: the half a minute or so that it took to run that race was the longest half minute of my life so far, and then the agony was prolonged when, in a heart-stopping finish – heart-stopping for me at least – Commutering Kid and another dog finished so close together that a photo finish was called. So I had to carry on sweating and praying a while longer – and then when it was announced that Commutering Kid had won I sunk down on my knees. Mary the cashier thought I'd gone bonkers.

After all the anguish, I was £300 up on the day. I gave Mary £100 – I hope she didn't think it was just to keep her quiet, though of course it was – then shoved the other £200 into my sock, before ringing up Head Office with my figures. Over all we took about £10,000 that day, whereas the shop's usual turnover for a Saturday was around £4,000, but that wasn't something I was going to start bragging about.

At 5.30 the two security men duly arrived to collect the takings and the film from the little camera which recorded every bet. At first they queried whether that final £1,100 bet might have been put through after the dog had won, but after they'd looked through the film which recorded all bets they were reassured that it had not. (I didn't tell them that had it been put through after time I would have been spared those few minutes of sweating ...)

Doubtless impressed by the day's total, they then asked who was the big punter who seemed to have been betting all afternoon. I said I didn't really know: I'd never seen him before, but I thought he might have been some local Irish car dealer.

I handed the keys back to the security guys, who said that they'd be in touch on Monday – and I thought it would be touch-your-toes time, and I'd be in for another Rhodes Boyson-style thrashing.

But when on the Monday morning I was duly phoned by head office, it was not to be fired or told to turn myself in at the local police station. They'd been so impressed by the turnover I'd generated in my day's stint as manager that they wanted to know whether I'd like to run a branch full time.

I gave them a two-word answer: NO, THANKS!

At this time I was making a few extra quid by clerking for bookmaker Georgie Edwards in the Silver Ring – the cheap enclosure – at Walthamstow dog track. One day a new tic-tac – one of those guys who wave their arms around to transmit money round the betting ring by using that mysterious sign language – arrived to work for a bookie on the end pitch. He was a large man, dressed in a huge cloak, and he'd arrived at the Stow riding a creaky old tricycle.

His manner of working was as eccentric as his dress: while furiously tic-tacking around the ring, he'd keep up a steady bellowing of 'Big one! Big one! Big one!' every time he made a transaction. At first we thought he was some sort of nutcase, but after a short while we came to appreciate that he was extremely good at the job. In fact I'd go so far as to say that he was one of the best tic-tacs I ever saw.

His name was John McCririck.

Nowadays Big Mac always bills himself as 'a failed book-maker', but he certainly wasn't a failed tic-tic. He was very good indeed.

By then I was back living with my parents. The one-room flat in Winchmore Hill which I shared with the rats was so dismal that after a couple of weeks I rang home in floods of tears, and my Mum came straight round and collected me. She never spoke a word of criticism or recrimination; she just kept repeating how pleased they were to have me back living at home.

But every penny I earned was going on betting, and gambling was becoming more and more like a disease. Of course, every now and again I'd win a few quid, but winnings would go straight back over the betting shop counter.

In those days the big 'coming of age' birthday was your twenty-first rather than the eighteenth it is today, and it's a measure of how low I'd sunk that I simply can't remember anything at all about my twenty-first. Did I have a party? What sort of presents did I get from Mum and Dad and sister Jacky? It was like a complete blackout, apart from gambling, gambling, gambling – and I knew that this just couldn't go on.

One day I decided that enough was enough. I looked up Gamblers Anonymous in the phone book, found that there was a meeting over in the Old Street area, and decided it was time to swallow my pride and go along.

The meeting was held in a grim mission hall, and when I went in the scene was pretty much as I'd expected. There were about twenty people sitting in a circle on plastic chairs, and when the meeting began it was all that confessional stuff: 'My name is Gary' – no surnames were ever revealed – 'and I'm addicted to gambling.'

There was a bloke named Harold, who on each of the first three occasions I went would solemnly declare: 'My name is Harold and I haven't had a bet for six years.' We all mumbled our approval of his strength of purpose, and told ourselves that we'd make Harold our role model, and follow his example in order to reform, etc. etc. Then we'd tell about our experiences: what we'd done to get the money for the next bet – beg, borrow, steal or earn – and how we were planning to escape from that terrible downward spiral just as soon as we could. Some of us might have really meant it, but most of us were lying – and of course we were still punting.

At the second meeting I told them that I hadn't had a bet since the previous week's session. This was a complete porky-pie, but I thought it was a suitable thing to say, even though I was very sceptical about what good the whole business was doing me.

The third meeting I attended finished a bit before nine o'clock, which fitted my schedule well. Harringay dog track was not far away, first race 7.45, last race 9.30 – and they used to open the gates before the last race to allow people to get away sharpish, and let in for free anybody who wanted to watch the 9.30 heat.

So after the meeting I nipped down to Harringay on the bus, and as I was waiting for the gates to be opened a hand clapped me on the back, and a voice behind me said: 'Hallo, son, how are you?' It was Harold – the very same Harold who not two hours earlier had been telling us that he hadn't had a bet for six years!

I'm aware that over the years Gamblers Anonymous has done a terrific amount of good for addicts, but I decided that it really wasn't for me, and I never went back.

I was now at rock bottom, and stayed there for the next few years, just about managing to keep body and soul together by doing all sorts of jobs.

One of these jobs was driving minicabs for a firm based at Oakwood tube station, one stop from the end of the Piccadilly Line and not far from Enfield. The company's boss, Jack Chadwick, must have bailed me out of financial meltdown a million times. When I was punting heavily I'd be asking him every day, 'Jack – got a score you could lend me?', and never once did he refuse. I could have been the best minicab driver in the world, but I'd never go home with so much as a penny in wages. It had all gone to the bookies.

Every Sunday I used to pick up a chap named Sterling, a fellow gambler and market trader who had a pitch in Leadenhall Market in the City of London. We got along very well, and one day he asked whether I fancied going to Spain for a week's fun with him and some of his mates. I said I had no money, but he offered to pay my air fare, so this was an offer I couldn't refuse.

We flew to Benidorm, and while we were booking in at the hotel a coach drove up and disgorged some forty girls from a firm in Glasgow called the Alliance Box Company. I'd had precious little interest in the opposite sex until then – they were too much of a distraction from gambling – but I liked one of these girls. Her proper name was Phylomena, which was so much of a mouthful that everyone called her Phyllis, and we spent a fair bit of our time in Benidorm together.

Neither of us wanted it to be just a holiday romance, so when we got back home we saw as much of each other as we could, given that we were 400 miles apart.

Phyllis lived in what was then a pretty rough area of Glasgow called Possilpark – so rough that one time a taxi refused to take me there, insisting that for cabbies it was strictly a no-go area. Despite that bad press, whenever I could – given the fragility of my finances, as I was continuing to fritter my money away gambling – I'd go up to see Phyllis.

I'd promised to be in Glasgow for our first New Year together, and somehow managed to scrape together £200 so that we could have a proper Hogmanay celebration. But then I made the mistake of deciding to get up there early and take in a few races at the Ashfield Greyhound Stadium.

Ever since cleaning up on those donkeys at Combe Haven I knew that you should arm yourself with a little local knowledge before steaming in, and as I'd never been to Ashfield before I decided to watch a few heats in order to get a feel for the track.

What struck me from the first few races was that in handicaps, every race was won by a dog who had started towards the back. (While in a horse race handicapping is done through varying the weights, in a dog race the differentials are made through staggering the traps, with the highest rated greyhound at the back and the lowest rated at the front.) I thought: this is easy – like taking candy from a baby. Time for me to get in on the action.

You'll hardly need telling that I left the stadium lucky still to have a fiver in my pocket. All thoughts of a lovely romantic New Year's Eve with Phyllis had gone out the window – or rather, into some Glasgow bookie's satchel – and I felt as bad as I ever had.

There was no point in trying to wriggle out of the situation, so I went straight to her house and confessed that I had blown the Hogmanay money. Rather than fly into a fit of rage and throw me out, as any sensible girl would have done, she calmly said that she had a few quid of her own put by, and we'd manage – which we did, going out and having a really good time.

Phyllis that New Year was just one example of how those around me and close to me have almost always treated my punting disasters: not just with sympathy, but with a determination to get things back on an even keel and move on. Many times – not least after Dettori Day – I have really found out who my friends are.

Not long later Phyllis and I split up, not on account of that New Year mess, but mainly because all that going up and down between Glasgow and London was getting too much for both of us.

It was around this time that a bookie I knew near Leather Lane named Mickey came along and asked whether I could clerk for him at a point-to-point the following weekend. I told him that although I knew about being a board man I had never clerked and wouldn't know what to do, but that wasn't a good enough excuse for Mickey.

'Can you read?'

'Yes.'

'Can you write?'

'Yes.'

'Then you can clerk. Be outside Holborn tube station at ten o'clock on Saturday morning.'

And that's how I first came to work on a racecourse pitch.

I duly turned up at Holborn tube, but there was no Mickey to be seen. About ten minutes later I was beginning to wonder what was going on and whether I should give up, when a black cab drew up to the kerb and from inside Mickey's voice shouted, 'Get in!' and off we went – five of us in all – in the direction of the point-to-point at Marks Tey in Essex.

In truth I can't say that we went straight there, for once we'd got out of the city someone suggested a brief stop at a nice looking country pub we were approaching. A pint of lager in that pub hit the spot, and we climbed back into the taxi – whose driver had sensibly stayed on water – and carried on towards Marks Tey.

And then we came across an even nicer looking country pub, and Mickey said we really ought to have a quick one in there, just to compare it with the other pub. Which we did – and then we were off again. I was a kid and not used to drinking in such quantities and at such speed, and after the second pint I was beginning to feel distinctly woozy.

Another few miles, and another pub – and then another and another and another, so that by the time we reached Marks Tey point-to-point course we must have visited eight or ten establishments. We set up the pitch in a very relaxed mood indeed.

That day was magical. The basic job of the bookie's clerk was to write down every bet in pencil on a large ledger, to record every bet but also to keep tabs on the bookmaker's liability for each race. That might sound simple enough, but it can be a very pressurised role when you're surrounded by punters clamouring to get on – and for me on my first day it was especially pressurised in another sense, on account of the ten pints of lager I'd consumed on the way there.

We stopped at every pub on the way back into London, and when Mickey's cab poured me out back at Holborn tube he gave me £80 in cash, my wages for the day. But even before I got that windfall, the whole experience had convinced me that being a bookmaker was what I wanted to do. I wouldn't go so far as to say that the day at Marks Tey changed my life, but it certainly gave me a real ambition for the first time. OK, it was not to be Prime Minister or an astronaut, or to ride the Derby winner, or to find a cure for cancer, but it was a real target. For the first time in my life I knew the direction I wanted to take.

And I was beginning to have a more normal relationship with the opposite sex.

Not long after finishing with Phyllis I started going out with a Jewish girl named Susan – not in any way to be confused with my wife Sue, please!

I first met her at Walthamstow dogs, where she'd gone with a friend who wanted to have a stall in Leather Lane market. Somebody pointed me out to them as the man to give advice, and we met up in a pub in Chingford – and then arranged to meet again rather higher up the social scale at the Epping Forest Country Club, where she arrived in this flashy white E-Type Jaguar, red leather seats and all.

After we'd got to know each other for a while, Susan encouraged me to take her E-Type when I was going off somewhere, as it was bound to impress the arse off anybody who set eyes on it. But the trouble was that I never held on to money long enough to keep putting petrol in it.

Somehow I managed to keep that from Susan, by simply pretending that I'd taken her car when I hadn't.

In due course a date was set for our wedding, which was to take place at the Reform Synagogue in Oakwood.

Everything was arranged. The invitations had been sent out, and all the preparations had been done, with one exception. I'd undertaken to convert to the Jewish faith, and that involved not only having to buy a whole pile of books which I was never going to read, but also making my way down to the local hospital about a week before the wedding to get myself circumcised.

Circumcised! That preyed on my mind no end. Night after night I'd wake up in a cold sweat in the early hours of the morning just thinking about it, and on the day before the appointment at Chase Farm Hospital I said to myself, 'I really don't fancy this one little bit', and there and then did what any sensible person would have done.

I did a bunk.

Stupidly, I didn't even tell my parents what I was going to do, and I really hadn't planned my escape in any detail. I was just going to strike out into the unknown.

First stop was hardly the unknown: Fontwell Park in West Sussex, where there was a race meeting that day. I took a train down there and managed to win something in the region of £700 – I couldn't have scarpered had I lost – then got a taxi to Weymouth and caught the ferry down to Jersey.

I felt more guilty than I can say over letting Susan and everyone else down in that way. But I did nothing to let them know where I'd gone, which I suppose just illustrates how blinkered, how selfish I'd become by then. I just tried to wipe everybody else out of my mind.

Jersey was just the place to lose myself for a while. I stayed there for the whole of the summer season, working every evening at a night club for holiday-makers called the Hawaiian in Portelet Bay. All done up in evening dress, I'd introduce the cabaret acts, which seemed to consist either of crooners or of girls gyrating in grass skirts – the waitresses were similarly attired in hula-hula skirts – and maintain some propriety when a male customer who had had one too many overstepped the mark with one of the girls. I was a becoming a big lad by then, and they tended not to argue with me.

(By the way, don't go looking for the Hawaiian in Portelet Bay: it was knocked down, and on the site is now a housing estate.)

It was the best job a gambler could have, because the Hawaiian Club didn't open until about eight in the evening, which meant that I could spend the afternoons – surprise, surprise – in the bookie's, gambling away the money I'd earned the night before. And the very best thing about Jersey was that, unlike in Britain at the time, there was no tax in betting shops.

In a strange sort of way I found that I was starting to enjoy life again. I loved the job at the Hawaiian Club. There were plenty of tips and drinks from the customers, and the stage shows allowed the showman in me to come out a bit. Just down from the club was a Butlin's Holiday Camp – one of the very first, I think – where I'd go for a drink after work.

But happy as I was with this routine, I knew it couldn't last for long, and that sooner or later I'd have to go back to Enfield and face the music. I'd had no contact whatsoever with my parents, and the more I thought about that, the worse I felt.

One day, after doing my money yet again in a Coombes betting shop, I told the manager of the Hawaiian Club that I'd be leaving straight away, and made directly for the ferry.

When I reached 900 Great Cambridge Road I rang the doorbell. After what felt like an age, the door was slowly opened, there was Mum, who was just able to whoop 'Gal – you're back!' before the tears started rolling down her face.

I knew I'd just backed the best winner of my life so far.

3

'Don't become a
bookie, Gal'

When they'd got over the shock of seeing the Prodigal Son returned, Mum and Dad sat me down on the sofa and listened while I told them where I'd been and what I'd been doing for all those months when they didn't know whether I was alive or dead. In the circumstances they were amazingly kind not to have a real go at me for disappearing like that.

Then it was their turn to tell me what a huge amount of trouble my going off had caused at their end. Susan had been distraught at the wedding being called off so close to the day, and they hadn't heard anything from her for ages.

Not long after I'd buggered off they'd been in touch with Phyllis in Glasgow to see if she knew where I was. She had no idea, of course, but they'd kept in touch with her all through that summer, and Mum told me to phone her and let her know I was still alive.

I did as I was told, which proved the rekindling of our relationship, and in 1977, when I was twenty-two, we were married. She moved down from Glasgow and we found a flat in Ranelagh Road in Tottenham, rent £6 per week.

At long last I was beginning to settle down, but life was still far from straightforward, and as often as not I had little idea where the rent was coming from.

Even when Phyllis got pregnant, I didn't seem able to keep on the straight and narrow as far as money was concerned. A few weeks before the baby was due, we started working out what essentials we'd need, and near the top of the list was a pram.

The trouble was, not only did I have no money to spend on a pram, but two weeks' rent on our Tottenham flat was due on the Monday and I was completely skint. So early on the Saturday morning I went along to Covent Garden market at Nine Elms to try and buy some flowers which I could then sell on. But by the time I got to the market there was nothing left.

Things were looking very grim, and then I noticed one of those huge dustbins, a sort of skip into which all the damaged and unsaleable flowers used to be dumped. I pulled myself up to take a gander over the top – I wasn't quite as well built then as I am now – and saw that someone had recently ditched about twenty boxes of gladioli in there.

They looked OK to me, so I clambered in and grabbed all twenty boxes, then made my way across London to the market in Exmouth Street, close to the Mount Pleasant sorting office. There I set up a little stall, and by lunchtime had cleared about £30. Keeping £12 aside for the rent, I went to the nearest betting shop and invested the rest in a Super Yankee – that is, a multiple bet involving five selections and consisting of twenty-six bets: ten doubles, ten trebles, five four-horse accumulators and one five-horse accumulator. The magnetic attraction of such a bet is that if all five come in you can win a huge amount for a small outlay, and even if four of the five oblige you'll get a serious return. But the chances of four or five of the horses winning is obviously small, so to bookmakers a bet like the Super Yankee is considered strictly for the mug punter.

No mug this time, though. On that memorable afternoon every horse won, and all of a sudden I was sitting on £480. So off Phyllis and I went to the Mothercare shop in Stratford, East London, and bought pram, cot, the lot – so that when our daughter Kelly arrived she had the best of everything.

That Super Yankee meant so much more than the higher-value winners later, because it meant that Kelly was not deprived from the moment of her birth. In lots of ways she and all the rest of my kids were deprived in later life, but at least I was able to give her a proper start.

Not long after she was born we moved out to South Ockendon in Essex, where we lived in a pretty unpleasant council flat, and after a few months we were on the move again – this time out to Milton Keynes.

I got my first job in a betting ring clerking two nights a week for bookmaker Derek – 'Del' – Borrows at Milton Keynes dog track, and as I was in employment we qualified for a council house: 42 Springfield Boulevard.

In 1978, when I was twenty-three, I thought that I knew enough about the betting business to take out a licence of my own. My Dad had always said to me: 'Don't become a bookie, Gal

– you won't last two weeks.' But I ignored that advice back then, and despite some well-known reverses, have never regretted it.

I applied for a licence to the Magistrates' Court at Stony Stratford, not far from Milton Keynes, and my application was far from the shoo-in I'd expected.

They asked me what experience I had, and – a crucial element in getting the application passed – how much money I had behind me. You were supposed to deposit a minimum of £10,000, to safeguard punters from the bookie welshing, and after I'd scraped together everything I could to raise the money for that, I had about a tenner to my name.

They also took into account character references and your police record, and wanted to quiz me about my conviction some years ago for being drunk and disorderly in Bridlington. Not only had I never been drunk and disorderly in Bridlington, I'd never even been to Bridlington – but the solicitor who was helping me with my application suggested that I didn't make too much of a fuss about that, and as it turned out the licensing panel didn't make any sort of issue of it.

The bottom line was that my application was approved and I got my licence, and I kicked off as a bookmaker in my own right at the flapping track at Nutts Lane in Hinckley. A flapping track staged unofficial greyhound racing: you could train a dog in your back garden and run it at flapping tracks, which weren't officially administered by the NGRC – the National Greyhound Racing Club, dog racing's equivalent of the Jockey Club in horse racing.

The dogs that were racing at Hinckley then were pretty well as good as the dogs you'd get running at Walthamstow or Harringay, but you could never be sure that somebody wasn't trying to pull a fast one by entering a decent dog under an assumed name, so that punters wouldn't know who he was. So you might run a Greyhound Derby winner and call him Matchstick – though of course there was no guarantee that another dog in the race named Rover wasn't the Derby winner in Scotland!

One of the other bookmakers at Hinckley was a man named Lesley Wootton, who was a dead ringer for the actor Bill Maynard. Bill himself lived somewhere nearby and was a keen punter at local tracks, and he based the character of Claude Jeremiah Greengrass in the television series *Heartbeat* on the bookmaker, which secretly pleased old Lesley no end. He was the salt of the earth, the sort of man who was always ready to lend you a few quid when you were on your uppers – though he liked to hand the money over with some comment like, 'Oh, these Cockney kids, they're all mouth and no trousers – they never have no money!'

The other person I associate closely with Hinckley is my old mate Gary Selby, for so long a familiar face on the At The Races satellite channel.

I first encountered Gary in a Coral's betting shop in Milton Keynes, not long after I'd moved there. I was sitting quietly doing my 28 five-pence forecast doubles or whichever exotic bet had taken my fancy that day, when I started talking to this man who turned out to be a very knowledgeable boy as far as anything to do with horses and dogs was concerned.

I asked him to come and clerk for me at Hinckley. He proved a natural, and before I knew it we were best mates.

All sorts of other scams and tricks went on at Hinckley.

For example, I had a dog named Exclusive Native, who whenever the money was down on his handsome nose never once failed to oblige. In fact he was more reliable than most human beings I've come across in my life. But every now and then we didn't want him to win, in order to get a better price when he was trying, and to slow him down we had little schemes like feeding him a sausage not long before the race. Not any old sausage, however, but a sausage with an aspirin concealed inside. That took the edge off him, I can tell you.

In those days I'd sometimes need to cash in Phyllis's Family Allowance and take the money to Hinckley dogs to get started, but as I got more experienced it was more and more unusual for me to have a losing day.

And I have a particularly soft spot for Hinckley because it was the only course where I ever had the bottle to offer even money about three dogs in the same race!

For me, those years were the great days of dog racing, which was much better supported back then when there were fewer rival attractions of an evening. There was the cinema or the pub but not a lot else, and for punters there was not much activity, as while there was a fair amount of evening racing in the summer, in those days betting shops were open only until the end of the afternoon.

Nowadays you can watch a dog race or a horse race in the betting shop until late in the evening, so why go out and get cold? Of course, there were some people like me who found the atmosphere of the track and the live action completely irresistible, but modern punters want a bit of comfort, and the shops are providing that.

I moved on from Hinckley to Warwick dogs, where one night I encountered a man called Arthur Cain, a night-club owner from Birmingham who loved his dog-racing and owned a few.

They used to have open races over a straight 100 yards, and we'd start the betting at 2-1 each of the six dogs, as we never knew in advance which was the 'buzzer'.

When I put the prices up for one of these races, Arthur was immediately on to us, asking for £800 to £400 on the 3-dog. I laid him a bet of £400 to £200, and marked trap 3 down to even money. He came straight back asking for an even £400, so I halved him again and went 2-1 on – at which point he had £400 to win £200.

Then I went fours on, so he had £200 to win £50. He just wouldn't be put off.

When the traps opened, the 3-dog carrying all Arthur's money practically fell out, while the others were much quicker into their stride – oh, what a lovely sight! I was adding up exactly how much I was taking off Arthur when the 3-dog finally started catching the others hand over fist. I was shitting myself, but mercifully the line came just in time, and the 3 was beaten a neck.

Then Arthur came up and let me into his little secret: 'You weren't to know this, son, but all six dogs in that race belong to

71

me, and five of them are family pets. Only the 3 had any chance.' I'd just got away with it.

Years later I met Arthur again at some betting forum, and the first thing he said to me was: 'Remember that race at Warwick, Gal?' As if I could ever forget …

The next dog track where I stood as a bookmaker – and my first under the auspices of the NGRC – was Leicester, which was managed by a fellow named Mick Whebel. A Londoner, Mick was a real ducker and diver, one of those blokes who would do anything for you, and for whom nothing was too unorthodox. No money changed hands when I was given my pitch at Leicester, but instead of a drink from me, Mick became the proud owner of a dozen crombie overcoats. God knows what I was doing with a spare dozen crombies: they must have fallen off a lorry!

When Leicester dog track closed down and Mick moved to Oxford, I moved with him. It was a very different place from Leicester, but there were still plenty of schemes to be tried.

At Oxford they ran greyhound hurdle races, which involved the dogs jumping obstacles a bit like racecourse hurdles but with brush tops, secured in the sand by stakes. Obviously a hurdle firmly pushed in would take a good deal more jumping than one more loosely secured, the top of which the dog could clip without losing much momentum.

One day a light-bulb suddenly turned on in my mind. Knowing which parts of the hurdles were more securely installed could prove very useful information, and I took to keeping a very close eye indeed on the groundsman whose job it was to put the obstacles in place.

In that way I'd become aware which dogs were going to have the advantage, and I'd price up the race accordingly.

This went on for year after year with nobody cottoning on to what I was doing – and I don't think even the hurdles man himself realised that for a few minutes each meeting he'd been the focus of my attention.

If anything was giving me the edge in the highly competitive world of bookmaking, it was that sort of thinking outside the box.

During the Oxford days, when I wanted to back a dog I couldn't easily get to a betting shop myself and have a decently hefty bet, so I'd use associates to have the money on for me. There were several men skilled in this unusual art, but the greatest of them all as far as the London betting shops were concerned was a cab driver named Dave Rossi.

People talk about geezers like Shakespeare or Michelangelo or Beethoven being great artists. Dave Rossi was one too. He had all sorts of schemes for getting the money on in such a way that the betting shop staff didn't realise what was going on – and I knew from my own experience at Hector Macdonald's that punters were always on the lookout for how to pull a fast one.

If we were targeting betting shops in the King's Cross area of London, one of Dave's schemes would be to pretend that he was a jeweller from Hatton Garden with a load of sovereign coins to sell. He'd take them into the betting shop in a briefcase and engage the staff in conversation about them, then leave them a few and say not to worry about paying him for them yet. He was going up to Sheffield to see his daughter at university there, he said, and would drop in again next week to see whether they wanted to buy them.

Before he returned the following week, the betting shop staff would have them valued and learn that they were worth sixty quid each – so when he turned up again and said he wanted thirty quid each they thought they were onto a bargain and would bite his hand off to buy a few more.

In that way he'd distract them from paying too much attention to whatever bet he was wanting to have on, and it hardly ever happened that he was knocked back when trying to put down a decent amount of money. The betting shop staff thought that they were pulling a little fast one on Dave, rather than the other way round!

Another of the roles he played was that of a moneyed but dim American tourist. He'd buy a copy of *USA Today* and tuck it under his arm. He'd get money bags from one of the big London casinos and put the cash in there, so that it looked as if he was playing up his winnings at roulette or whatever. He'd speak in an American accent and use American terms when asking for a bet, like 'Box' instead of Forecast. And generally he'd play the role of the dumb Yank.

If he was trying to get the money on in one of the big chain betting shops, as likely as not the manager would phone head office and say: 'We've got an American in who wants to have such and such a bet, but he's obviously a casino man' – that is, a man who loves to gamble on anything and probably knows nothing in particular about horses or dogs.

Dave's timing was exquisite. If a race was off at 2.30, he'd go into the shop at 2.24, having carefully worked out how long it would take to do his little act and get the money down. He'd then nip out to where he'd left his black cab – though on one occasion a betting shop manager intrigued by this strange American followed him out to the street, and Dave had to walk several blocks before he could shake him off. He couldn't be seen getting back into his cab!

Those days at Oxford dogs were some of the happiest of my life. Other young people go up to that famous seat of learning to study in posh colleges like Christ Church or Balliol, but beyond a shadow of a doubt I learned more at Oxford than they ever do.

It was not all plain sailing, and for a while I was banned from betting there in the afternoons. Curiously, this banning was mentioned in an article in *Punch* magazine years later in 1997 – an article which, though unsigned, sums up the issue quite well:

> *Wiltshire first made a name for himself eight years ago. He used to make a book from one of the five or six on-track pitches allocated by the stadium management. At the time, one of the big off-course betting shop chains had a habit of 'investing' in the on-course market there when they wanted to shorten up the price of a fancied dog. Five hundred pounds of the big firm's money would generally be enough*

to see the on-course bookies cut the odds to as low as even money. But not Wiltshire. He refused to play.

'Take me on,' he told the big boys. 'Or take the punters on. I'm calling my own prices'. So if the ring went to evens, he'd go to 2-1. If they went to threes he'd go out to 7-2. And so on. Perhaps not incidentally, only six months later Gazza was elbowed, or otherwise deleted from the list of Oxford bookies. But by the time he'd left he'd built up a hero's reputation with the punters and further dented the credibility of the big chains.

That's a fair account. If I laid a grand at 3-1 to a dog-owner and didn't then shorten the price, that was up to me, and I wasn't going to be bullied by the chains. But the big boys had the muscle – hence the ban. I was allowed to bet at Oxford in the evenings, though, as back then betting shops weren't open in the evenings and so the chains had little reason to shorten one up.

Then an opportunity came up at Milton Keynes, where I stood for some twenty years (and handed the pitch over to my eldest son Nicky).

I started off by sharing the pitch with the great bookie Johnny Earl, one of the cleverest cookies ever born and a man who became a close friend as well as a mentor in the weird and wonderful ways of the betting ring. I absorbed a huge amount about the tricks of the trade from him, while further along the line were other great characters, including one bookie who was rumoured to be the local cattle rustler!

To make my pitch distinctive and attract attention, I special-
ised in betting without the favourite, and with Gary Selby as my
clerk and trusty right-hand man, was soon making a very decent
living indeed.

Although standing as a bookmaker was taking up most of
my time, I still liked to work the markets whenever I could – to
keep a sort of hold on my roots, perhaps.

One day I was selling flowers, bulbs and the like at the market
on Canvey Island, near Southend, when a bloke named Bob
Wheatley drove up in his Rolls Royce. He'd done very well for
himself, had Bob, and owned a few racehorses (the best known
of which was Baron Blakeney, who won the Triumph Hurdle at
Cheltenham in 1981).

His racing colours were red and yellow, and he asked me
whether I could get him two thousand bulbs, one thousand in
red and the other thousand in yellow, as he wanted to make
some magnificent floral display at his house.

No problem, I told him, and quoted him four pence a bulb.
Fine, he replied – and when he said that he'd be back at the next
market to pick them up I was well chuffed, as two thousand
times four pence was a nice little sum of money in those days.

So I went off to Nine Elms and found the main man who
dealt in bulbs. 'I need 1,000 red bulbs and 1,000 yellow,' I told
him: 'How much would they be?'

'About 3½ pence each,' he told me, 'but I'll have to get them
in.' Then he added: 'But I can do you a sort of reddy pink tulip
bulb for a penny each – and you can have them now.' He showed

me what they looked like when they came up, and they were a pretty horrible colour – but they gave me an idea.

So I bought two thousand of the things and went home and divided them into two large wooden boxes – then wrote 'RED' with a thick felt-tip pen on one box and 'YELLOW' on the other.

The next week Bob Wheatley came and collected them, and seemed well satisfied with the deal – though I was never to find out whether he remained quite so satisfied when they all came up the same colour, as I'd decided I'd better give Canvey Market a wide berth for a while …

Betting at the Midlands dog tracks was going well. I was really a tuppeny-ha'penny bookmaker, but I was never completely satisfied with my lot, and decided that the sensible way to expand was to get a rails pitch on a racecourse.

The whole point of rails bookmakers was that, for some obscure reason of history or traditional racecourse snobbery, betting (except for the Tote) was not usually allowed in the Members' Enclosure of a racecourse. So some bookies, including representatives of what were then the Big Four – Ladbrokes, William Hill, Coral and Mecca – stood with people from the leading independent firms inside the Tatts (that is, general) enclosure right on the fence dividing that area from the Members', and offered prices to Members' punters over the rail. Some cash changed hands, but a great deal of the business was done on credit.

For the big chains, betting on the rails was a way of collecting intelligence. They were, in effect, spies. Say they knew that a punter's regular stake was never more than £100, but that in the next race he had a horse of his own running and he wanted to stake £1,000, that told its own story. At the very least, that horse was 'off'!

Betting on the rails was all very discreet, so much so that back then bookies did not even have a board displaying the prices. You'd advertise your prices by shouting them out – literally calling the odds – and you'd rarely give out a ticket. So much was done on trust, and by betting with people – including the other bookmakers – that you knew.

On the rails was where you found the big layers who would take a large bet, and the high rollers would always bet with the big boys rather than a little tiddler, and unknown small boy – OK, not that small – from the Midlands.

Trust between punter and bookmaker was so much at the root of the rails business that you had to put down a bond of £20,000 before you could get a pitch – and you needed two securities of £20,000 each beyond that, just to get started. At that time being a rails bookmaker was a really privileged position, like a member of an exclusive club, whereas it feels nowadays as if anybody can bet on the rails.

The first rails pitch I was granted on a racecourse was at Perth, north of Edinburgh. Perth is the most northerly course in Great Britain and one hell of a long way from Milton Keynes, but it's well worth making the effort to get there, as this neat little jumping track in the grounds of Scone Palace, right by the River Tay, has an atmosphere all its own.

I've no idea how the local Scottish bookmakers felt about this loud-mouthed Cockney from the Midlands suddenly appearing in their ranks, but as far as I was concerned getting a pitch up there meant that at least I had a foot in the door.

From that beginning I started to further build up the business, and my second racecourse pitch was almost as far from Perth as it was possible to be: Folkestone in Kent. Here I decided that it would be more profitable to bet in the Silver Ring – the cheap enclosure – than on the rails, and I was proved right: although stakes in the Silver Ring tended to be significantly smaller than in Tatts or on the rails, there was a much bigger volume, which made the effort to go down there well worth while.

The next opportunity was again in Scotland, at the leading Scottish racecourse Ayr, where the two big fixtures of the year – for the Scottish Grand National in April and the Ayr Gold Cup in September – proved highly profitable.

My life was increasingly dominated by having to drive very long distances, but at least I could truthfully claim in the slogan displayed on my rails board: 'From Folkestone to Ayr, Wiltshire's there!'

4

'Come on, my son!'

usiness was expanding, and so was our family, with Kelly being followed by her brothers Nicky and Ross. But all that travelling around the country was unsurprisingly putting a strain on my relationship with Phyllis. Things got rougher and rougher between us, and we eventually split up in 1987. It was not so much my compulsive gambling which drove a wedge between us – I was always much more successful as a bookmaker than as a punter – but more the bookmaking life in general.

I'd be off at the crack of dawn to drive to some far-flung course, and I wouldn't get back until late at night – and as often as not would stay away, leaving Phyllis to cope with the children on her own and without any assistance whatsoever from me, other than bringing in the money.

Had I been more considerate I would have made sure that I could devote more time to the family, and over the last few years, with all three of the children I had with Phyllis now grown up, I'm only too acutely aware of what a terrible father I was to them. Yes, I was bringing in enough for them to have a reasonably comfortable existence, but I never – ever – devoted to them the amount of time that I should have done, and the guilt from that will be with me for ever.

I've always had a problem with what people call love. It's hard to love anybody when you've come home after having a really bad day at the races. You walk in the door and all of a sudden you have to change your mood, to act a part. Even in the bleakest days, I always used to put a Chas and Dave tape on in the car when driving home, and turn the volume up as loud as it would go. Despite the racket, that used to calm me down, and I was reasonably human again by the time I walked in the door, though careful not to show any particular emotion, win or lose.

But when I'd go to bed, I'd toss and turn, unable to sleep because of what had happened that day and what might happen the next day.

When I left school they said that I'd achieved just two 'O'-levels: one for gambling and the other one for finding fish and chip shops. My life took an unexpected turn when, not long after the split from Phyllis, I decided that I fancied a bit of skate one evening and walked into Reggie's Fish Bar in Milton Keynes – and into the life of a lady queuing in there with her sister for a little snack. They were on their way home after a session at Weight Watchers, so were ordering fish but no chips!

I was to live with Jackie – who, like so many of the other people in my life, was a florist – for seven years or so (although we never married), and our son Danny was born in August 1985. At one point Jackie had a flower shop named Valentine's Flowers in the Gray's Inn Road near Holborn, and for a while business there was very brisk. Then when some of the local businesses like the *Sunday Times* started moving away things started to get much harder, and eventually we had to close it down.

At this time I liked nothing better than to make a book at a point-to-point. I wouldn't take a vast amount of money – though you'd be surprised how thick a bet some of those 'between the flags' chaps liked – but I loved the atmosphere, and the differences between the various venues meant that each and every one was a fresh adventure.

One of the great point-to-pointing families in the south was the Balding clan, whose horses ran often at courses like Larkhill, Barbury, Kingston Blount and Tweseldown. Ian Balding, of course, trained the great 1971 Derby and Arc winner Mill Reef and the amazing sprinter Lochsong, but whatever the attractions of Flat racing at the very highest level, more than anything he loved riding in point-to-points, and was still doing so at what I might politely call an advanced age.

A Balding point-to-point horse for whom I have an especially fond regard was Ross Poldark. Ian won several races on him, and in 1983 they finished fourth in the Fox Hunters' Chase at Liverpool. Ian rode him again in the 1985 race, when the then fourteen-year-old fell quite early in the race.

I was making a book at the Vine and Craven point-to-point at Hackwood Park on Easter Monday 1987 when Ross Poldark provided a first ever point-to-point ride for Ian's daughter Clare, who like the horse was sixteen years old! The daughter of another great trainer was riding in the same race: Amanda

Harwood, whose dad Guy had the previous year won all sorts of big races with the great Dancing Brave. Ian Balding wrote in his autobiography:

Both Guy Harwood and I had come to Hackwood Park for the ladies' open, where our daughters were riding against each other, rather than going to Kempton where we both had rather more important runners on the Flat.

The conditions were appalling after torrential rain, and cars were stuck everywhere trying to get into the course. The stewards at the meeting even came and asked Guy and me if we felt it was safe to race. Knowing that our girls were on two very experienced jumpers we both said, 'Yes, of course, it's perfectly safe,' and the meeting went ahead. There was a third runner but Amanda (now Perrett) and Clare had a wonderful race with each other, with Amanda finishing just ahead on her slightly younger horse. On pulling up she was thrilled to have won, but knew she was in for a bollocking from her father for allowing Clare to get up on her inside at the last bend! Both fathers were extremely proud of their daughters and also of their wonderful old horses, who had taken them safely round in those desperate conditions.

I often wondered what heights 'Poldarkle', as our family used to call him, might have reached as a chaser if we had found him four or five years earlier. He was without doubt the most brilliant jumper of a fence that I ever rode, and

I do not think I was ever happier in my life than when bowling along in front making the running on him in those point-to-points at Tweseldown.

And I don't think that *I* have ever been happier in my life than when pricing up a race in which Ross Poldark was running. When that old boy was in the line-up I could lay the other runners all day, and we knew that dinner on the way home – prawn cocktail for the starter, a nice juicy sirloin steak for the main course and Black Forest Gateau to finish up – would be on Ross Poldark. God bless him!

It was around this time that I was making a book one Saturday at the Whaddon Chase point-to-point at Great Horwood, near Bletchley in Buckinghamshire, when I noticed nearby a beautiful property named Warren House, which by chance was for sale.

I was flush enough at the time and got straight on to the estate agent, saying that I wanted to buy it. The lady at the agents said that there were other people interested and I hadn't even had a good look round it, let alone get a survey and go through all that palaver, but I wouldn't be put off, and first thing on the Monday went round to the office, signed on the dotted line and paid in full. It was like buying sweets in a shop.

Warren House was a superb place to live. We converted one part of the stable block into a snooker room and another part into kennels for our dogs.

But I was not to live there for very long. Like Phyllis before her, Jackie was eventually forced to give up the unequal struggle and we parted. I'll never forget taking a call in my car a few years ago while driving down to Folkestone races. It was our son Danny, telling me that Jackie was very ill and in a hospice near Milton Keynes. I got off the motorway at the next junction, headed back north and went straight to the hospice, where she was in a shocking condition. She died not long afterwards.

I was making a good few quid, but what gave the business a more than handy cash injection was when Johnny Earl and I jointly backed Norton's Coin to win the 1990 Cheltenham Gold Cup at 200-1 – a grand each way for each of us with a well-known Northampton bookie named Con Wilson.

Con was one of the great layers. I'd first met him a few years earlier, after Johnny had told me that there was a bookmaker in Northampton who could be guaranteed to lay a good bet if you could get his confidence.

I decided to go and see this man, but thought I'd play a little game. Before setting off for Northampton I poured the contents of a bottle of Johnnie Walker whisky all over me – there was a little bit less of me then than there is now – and rubbed it into my skin, so that when Con met me I'd be smelling of the hard stuff and, he'd no doubt be thinking, in no state to be behaving rationally.

I had £40,000 cash in my pocket and after I'd lurched upstairs into his office a load of notes spilled out onto the floor. He must have thought I was a right prat, even more so when I said that I wanted the whole lot on some horse who was about to run at Folkestone and was expected to go off at something like 8-1 on.

He and his assistant counted out the money while I woozily rolled around in the chair, still pretending to be three sheets to the wind, and he took the bet. The horse won, but I declined to take the money there and then, and instead – before they poured me into a taxi – I set up a deposit account with Con.

Sadly he died a while ago, but he was a proper bookmaker, and it was he who laid me the 200-1 about Norton's Coin.

I've always believed in having a hefty each-way bet when the time is right, and Norton's Coin seemed – to me at least – to have a serious chance of getting in the frame. Although he came from a tiny yard – his trainer Sirrell Griffiths was a dairy farmer in a village near Carmarthen and had only three horses in training – Norton's Coin had got some good form in the book, and at 200-1 was stonking each-way value.

All the attention that year was on Desert Orchid, who had won the Gold Cup in appalling conditions the year before, since when he'd only been beaten once, when giving lumps of weight away all round in a handicap. Dessie's pre-Cheltenham race had been the Racing Post Chase at Kempton Park, when he carried top weight of 12st 3lb and turned in a brilliant performance to beat Delius. He seemed in the best shape he'd ever been in, and although Cheltenham was far from his ideal course, he was now being ridden by the great Richard Dunwoody (his Gold Cup-winning jockey Simon Sherwood had retired) and he went off odds-on jolly to win a second Gold Cup.

Norton's Coin, on the other hand, went off at 100-1 – though he wasn't the complete outsider: 'the rag', as we describe a no-hoper in the betting ring, was a horse called The Bakewell Boy who had a starting price of 200-1. The *Racing Post* didn't mention Norton's Coin at all in its race preview. The *Sporting Life* did mention him – calling him a 'no-hoper'. And I was later told that the Cheltenham racecard that day wrote him off as 'more of a candidate for last place than first.'

By then Desert Orchid was a real national treasure, and crowds flocked to Cheltenham on the Thursday of the National Hunt Festival – Gold Cup afternoon in those days – to see their favourite horse.

I should have been with them – I'd been at Cheltenham for the previous two days of the Festival – but didn't make it, and the reason why is a bit bizarre.

I was staying with Gary Selby, Del Borrows and a few others at a country club hotel a few miles from the racecourse, and we were having a good time – until, that is, on Gold Cup morning, just before we were about to set off for the track, the manager got into some sort of argument with Selby about an unpaid bill or something, and they blocked in our car in the car park to stop us from escaping!

We gave a bit of thought to tunnelling out – which might have had its drawbacks in the case of the two Garys – and having rejected that idea, tried to find a taxi to take us to the course. But by then it was far too late, and although everything got sorted out about the supposedly unpaid bill, by then we had no chance of getting to the races in time. So we settled down in the hotel bar, ordered a decent lunch and a few drinks, and watched the Cheltenham action on the telly.

The Gold Cup may have been all about Desert Orchid, but as they came into the home straight two of his rivals seemed to be going better: Toby Tobias, ridden by Mark Pitman for his mum Jenny, and – believe it or not – Graham McCourt on Norton's Coin.

You can imagine how this sight was going down with the gang of us watching the race in the bar of that hotel. We were starting to raise the roof as they cleared the second last, and there was still one more fence to go.

Halfway up the straight Dessie could find no more, which left Toby Tobias and Norton's Coin to go at it hammer and tongs up the hill, with me screaming Graham McCourt home. That pull up the Cheltenham hill from the last had never seemed longer, but Norton's Coin dug deep, then deeper still, and stride by stride Norton's Coin got the better of Toby Tobias. He pushed his head in front shortly before the line and won by three quarters of a length.

He was the longest priced winner in the race's history – and he'd improved my cash flow to the tune of a handy six-figure sum.

The reaction of some gloomy sods was to question whether I'd ever get paid in full, but they didn't know Con Wilson, who was as straight a bookmaker as you'd ever meet and of course paid up without blinking.

And on the strength of our winnings, Johnny Earl and I both bought villas in a lovely complex in Portugal, very close to the Pennina Golf Resort on the Algarve, which had been built by a Northampton builder we knew. It had a satellite dish almost as big as one of the villas, and for the next few years Portugal was a glorious place to escape from the rat race and spend a few days watching sport from around the world, day and night, and sunning myself into the bargain.

Not for long enough, though.

Another nifty piece of punting in the early 1990s involved holes in one in golf.

Gary Selby and I used to go all over Europe to golf tournaments, and we came up with a plan to make a few quid by betting on a player – any player, not a particular one – getting a hole in one over the four days of the competition.

From studying each round closely, we'd worked out that the true odds of any hole in one in a four-day professional golf tournament is around even money. But other people – and especially amateur golfers – thought that the odds must be something much bigger, anything up to 100-1. In betting terms, getting 100-1 about an even money chance was like shooting fish in a barrel.

The bookies would take bets on holes in one until 1pm on Thursday, the first day of the tournament. We'd target a betting shop near where the tournament was being held – always an independent, where the manager would be his own man and would have no head office to phone every time some punter came in wanting to make even a slightly unusual bet.

Then on the morning of the first day we'd put on Slazenger jumpers – nice touch that, I thought! – and wander into the bookie's shop and engage the manager in conversation about the event which was just starting. If the manager was himself a golf nut, we might happen to work into the conversation the fact that the other day one of us had had our first ever hole in one, and he'd think you were just stringing him along, as he'd never had one.

One of us would ask, as casually as you like, about the odds on there being a hole in one during that week's tournament. The manager would answer along the lines of, 'Oh, I don't know – something like 100-1?', and we were in.

This was completely legal and honest, a classic – if admittedly rare – case of the punter for once being much more alert and informed than the bookmaker, and for a few years we made it a very lucrative line, especially on the occasions when we were able to double up with a hole in one in some other tournament.

In 1992 there was a bit of a hoo-hah when another punting duo known as 'The Quality Street Gang' cleaned up big by betting on holes in one and some bookmakers refused to pay out. But The Two Garys were there first.

And one of those Garys – me – worked out a lovely scheme with Johnny Earl one year when the Open Golf was being held at Lytham St Annes.

Some of the independent betting shops in the Midlands used to put up 'Super Soccer' sheets of prices on football matches, and these sheets were delivered to the shops on Tuesday mornings. So with the Open about to start, Johnny and I produced a sheet of prices for the big tournament under the name Fairway Golf –

with our own prices, and including holes in one, naturally – and sent them to those independent shops, to arrive on Monday. The staff duly put them up along with all the other bumph which adorns the walls of betting shops, and over the next couple of days we'd go into those shops and get some wagers down on the golf with the luxury of betting at prices we ourselves had drawn up.

On one occasion, to give the shop manager the impression that I was just a mug punter looking for a casual bet, I dressed up in painter's overalls before I went in – and having got on, had to engage in a lengthy conversation with manager about the nearby house that I was helping do up!

With things going so well, it was time to indulge myself in something which for so long had been a complete pipedream – owning horses.

I'd already owned a good few greyhounds, but owning a racehorse is an operation of a completely different order. For one thing, it's much more expensive, but if you go in with a canny trainer you can have the occasional moment of triumph to go along with the much more frequent setbacks.

My first horse was a mare named Vado Via. She was originally trained by Lynda Ramsden, who with her husband Jack formed one of the shrewdest husband-and-wife racing teams of them all. When they went for a touch, boy did they go for a touch!

In September 1991 Vado Via, then a three-year-old, ran in a claiming race – that is, a very lowly race after which any runner may be 'claimed' by someone else for an advertised sum – on the Flat at Leicester. I was there that day and was so taken by Vado Via in the paddock that I kept a special eye on her during the race – in which, ridden by Dean McKeown, she finished fifth, though not beaten a very long way by the winner.

I got that shrewdie trainer David Wintle, whom I'd known for a good while and whose very sharp son James had worked with me at Oxford dogs, to claim her for £6,000. The claim was successful, and I was the proud owner of a three-year-old filly by Ardross, who had won two Gold Cups at Ascot in the early 1980s when ridden by Lester Piggott and damn nearly won the Prix de l'Arc de Triomphe. Vado Via's dam Brigado was a daughter of the very great Brigadier Gerard, the horse who had been beaten only once in eighteen races in the 1970s. So whatever her form, my new acquisition was bred well enough to win a few races.

Our plan was to send her hurdling, and she first ran over the sticks at Ludlow just nine days after the Leicester race. She started 15-8 second favourite but finished a well beaten fourth of six runners. We had no intention of hurrying her along, and were not put off when she finished eighth at Windsor at 16-1 and then sixth at Haydock Park at 20-1.

We then went to Bangor-on-Dee for a selling hurdle. She started 7-2 joint favourite and only had to be driven out by Tony Carroll to win handily.

This owning game was beginning to agree with me, and more success was to come, as Vado Via was then second three times and third once before winning again at Exeter, when she was ridden by the then amateur jump jockey Richard Davis.

Richard was a lovely lad, a charming and really stylish rider for whom the future looked very promising indeed. He went on to become a professional jockey and was quietly making a name for himself when in July 1996 he was riding a complete no-hoper in a steeplechase at Southwell. At the first fence the horse barely left the ground, turning a cartwheel onto the landing side and pile-driving Richard into the turf. He died in hospital a few hours later, and I heard the news late that evening. It was one of the saddest days of my racing life.

Vado Via got beaten in her next two races, but in November 1992 David identified a conditional jockeys' handicap hurdle at Haydock Park as a likely target, and booked Warren Marston, later a first-rate jump jockey but back then just a highly promising youngster, for the ride. The filly was in very good order, and we knew that this was a day to get the money down on course.

I arranged to go up to Haydock on the morning of the race with David and Warren, and with Gary Selby driving, we set off up the M6 expecting a decent payday.

Then we hit the mother of all traffic jams: the motorway was shut because, we learned later, holes had appeared in the surface further up. Must have been the Haydock bookies trying to scupper our plan …

All traffic was being diverted off the M6, and it soon dawned on us that we were going to be very hard pressed indeed to get to Haydock in time: in time for Warren to clock in by the

What a fine figure of a man!

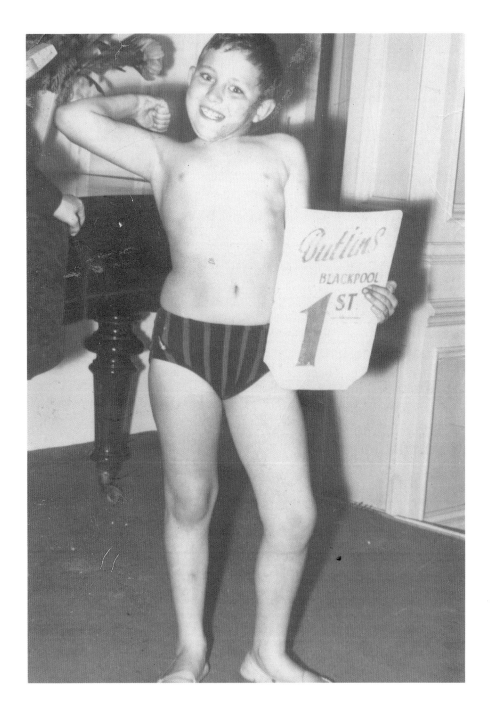

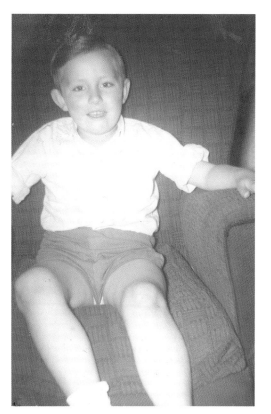

Young Gal: *Opposite*, after winning the Junior Tarzan competition at Butlin's in Blackpool. *This page, clockwise from above*: Taking a rest; with Mum and Dad at Blackpool; a happy-go-lucky nine-year-old; with my best friend at primary school, Michael Few.

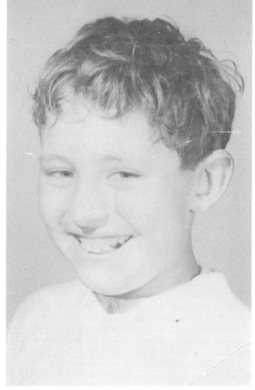

Above: With Bentico and jockey Amanda Sanders in 1995 after yet another win.

Below: Come on, my son! Suivez and 3-pound claimer Jim Culloty – who was to win three Gold Cups and a Grand National – winning the Ladbroke Hurdle at Ascot in April 1996.

Above: Snogging local resident Roger Brooke at the Gay Pride Day at Brighton. I won't tell you what we got up to later …

Below: Vinnie Jones at Oxford dogs with one arm around my missus – I wasn't inclined to make something of it with Vinnie – and the other around legendary greyhound trainer Ginger McGee.

Above: Two of the greats, and great mates: Dave Rossi (left), a genius among putting-on merchants; and Peter Houghton, who still has the bruise from when I punched him on Dettori Day.

Below: Sue and I settling down for a little light snack in Gran Canaria.

Above: The converted garage (on the left) where we lived after selling up to help pay the Dettori debts … but (*below*) Dettori Day started the process which would make me well known as 'The Belly from the Telly'.

WONDERS

Gary
WILTSHIRE
"The Belly from the Telly"

SEVEN
2 TWO
EIGHT

Ptd by WRS Bradford BD2 2HL 01274 770733

ORDER N° M 412 /Gw

CORAL   DEPARTMENT,
Glebe House, Vicarage Drive,
Barking, Essex IG11 7NS

Telephone: 081-591 5151
Facsimile: 081-591 8761

OFFICIAL ORDER

Ref: G Wiltshire/On Course

Period ending 28 Sept. 1996

Page 1

Date	Stake	Details	Balance
28 Sept.	£40,000	Fujiyama Crest @ 7-2	£140,000
28 Sept.	£20,000	Fujiyama Crest @ 7-2	£210,000
28 Sept.	£30,000	Fujiyama Crest @ 3-1	£300,000
28 Sept.	£10,000	Fujiyama Crest @ 3-1	£330,000
28 Sept.	£40,000	Fujiyama Crest @ 11-4	£440,000
28 Sept.	£10,000	Fujiyama Crest @ 5-2	£465,000
28 Sept.	£10,000	Fujiyama Crest @ 9-4	£487,500

AMOUNT DUE FOR FINAL SETTLEMENT   £487,500

Don't you hate it when bills arrive? …

required time, that was, and in time for us to get the money down. So David phoned ahead to Haydock and asked if they had a conditional jockey there without a ride in this particular race. As luck would have it, we were offered the services of Barry Murtagh, a promising Irish lad who happened to be free. So we booked him and, over the phone from the car, David gave him his riding instructions: hold her up, and don't make your move until the last possible moment.

The race was due off at 2.10, and I can tell you there was some serious sweating going on as the time ticked away. God knows what the other drivers thought as Gary tried every trick in the book – and plenty not in the book – to get past them.

I used to think that Selby was the worst driver in the world, but that day he drove like a man inspired and really saved our bacon. Don't ask me how he did it – his detour seemed to involve driving down every street in Wigan and through several back gardens in Warrington – but somehow, just when I was despairing of ever seeing Haydock Park again, we turned a corner and there was the racecourse. At 2.04 we screeched into the owners' and trainers' car park. I expect the scorch marks are still there.

Even before we'd come to a halt, I was out of that car like a dog from the traps at Walthamstow, and I sprinted (or did the nearest to sprinting that I could at the time) into the betting ring.

In the morning papers Vado Via had been as short as 3-1, but as there had been no money for her at the track her price had been allowed to drift to around twice that. I made a beeline for the three main bookies there – Pat Whelan, Tom James and Lesley Steele – and banged in three bets of five grand each at 6-1 – and the very instant that the third wodge of money landed in the bookie's satchel, they were off. It was as if God had decided to be nice to me that day – though at Ascot not many years later the Almighty was to take a different line.

Sweating heavily after my dash from the car park, I joined David and Gary in the stand to watch the race. Coming out of the back straight Vado Via was cruising along just behind the leaders and going as well as anything. It was just a question of the young lad keeping her covered up and letting her go on as late as possible.

Once the field had turned for home, with about half a mile to go, to our horror he eased her forward, so that by the second last hurdle – far too soon, we thought – she was clear. She was still clear at the last, but on the run-in seemed to be idling – but then kept going well enough to win by two and a half lengths.

We drew the readies immediately and drove straight home, with a good few quid more in the car than we'd had on the way up, and at a more leisurely pace.

That was a very special day, but I had plenty of fun with others, and having a few horses – and thus a direct line to a trainer or two – came in very useful when in the early 1990s I had a telephone tipping line, when punters could phone up and get the benefit of my wisdom for the day's sport, dogs as well as horses.

On one occasion a horse I owned was entered in a selling hurdle at Fontwell Park, which after the final declarations was going to have a field of only three runners. I knew that my horse had little chance as the going was not in his favour, but we decided to run him as the money for finishing third was worth collecting – and in addition I could turn the situation to my advantage through the tipping line: I recommended that the bet of the day was to combine the other two runners in reverse forecasts. Sure enough, mine finished third. Result!

The agreement for subscribers to the tipping line was that for every winner – and there were a good few – they would pay me the winning odds to £40: so if I tipped a 2-1 winner, they'd send me £80. Perfect: the punters were happy to get proper inside information, and I was happy to cash their cheques and postal orders.

I'd been going through a purple patch on the tipping line – something like eleven winners out of twelve selections – when David Wintle and I decided to go for a touch in a selling hurdle at Sedgefield in December 1993.

David had in his yard a horse named Damcada, an Irish-bred novice hurdler who ran under the ownership of E4 Racing. He'd finished out with the washing in novice hurdles at Towcester and Warwick earlier in the season and would not be hotly fancied for the Sedgefield race, but we knew that he was ready for it. So the advice on the tipping line was to get on at the first betting show, and we were so confident that we put Damcada up as a double bet: that is, subscribers were told to have twice their usual stake on him – and, of course, would have to pay us double the commission when he won.

Damcada opened up at 8-1 for what without our involvement would have been a very weak betting heat, and with all our money on at the first show that price did not last a minute. He started at 5-1, and would have been much shorter than that had there not been a hot favourite in the form of the Gary Moore-trained Raggerty, who was on a three-timer.

Ridden by the ever-reliable Warren Marston, Damcada took the lead from the start and never for a moment looked like being headed, staying out stoutly from two hurdles out to win cosily.

But there was a sting in the tail.

Since Damcada had been a doubly strong selection, by the terms of their subscription tipping line punters were obliged to cough up £640 – eight times £80 – in return for that gilt-edged advice, and only about half of the 180-odd subscribers did so. For the first time, it dawned on me that while they weren't fussed at sending £80 for a 2-1 winner, creaming £640 off their winnings for the poor bloke who'd tipped them the winner was too much!

Of course, those who didn't pay weren't given any more tips so they were doing themselves down in the long run. We'd had it off and we'd won a nice amount ourselves, but the whole episode left a sour taste in my mouth. I decided that henceforth I'd keep my red-hot information to myself, and closed down the tipping line.

In 1995 we pulled off a nice little gamble with a horse I owned called Montague Dawson, trained at Melton Mowbray by Norma Macauley, with whom I had plenty of horses over the years and who, while never in the Premier League of trainers who won big races, was an absolute genius at getting one ready for a race on the all-weather.

I'd bought the horse after he'd run way down the field in a selling race at Folkestone on August 1994, his second unsuccessful outing as a two-year-old for Newmarket trainer Michael Bell, and when early in 1995 he started coming good on the gallops we thought we could have some fun with him.

The race chosen was at Southwell in February, and given his complete lack of promise as a juvenile he was expected to go off at a long price. We entered another horse named Tynron Doon in a race at Market Rasen the same afternoon. Norma was going to go to Southwell to saddle Montague Dawson, while her husband Don was deputed to go with the other horse to Market Rasen – and Don hadn't been told about the serious money being on Montague Dawson.

In order not to give anybody in the betting ring the impression that Montague Dawson was the order of the day, I made my mind up not to go to Southwell (what was the point if the horse had no chance at all?), and instead went off to Market Rasen with Don, though not before I'd arranged for a friend – I can't remember whether it was the legendary Dave Rossi – to go round a series of independent betting shops and in each one have £40 to win on Montague Dawson. In all, we had on about three grand each way at 20-1.

(The point of spreading bets around many shops, of course, is (a) that if you tried to wager a very big stake in one shop you'd almost certainly be knocked back or downright refused, and (b) the placing of a large single bet raises suspicions in the big bookmakers, who are constantly monitoring where the money is going in their shops, that a horse is fancied by those in the know. By spreading the money around several independents, alarm bells would not be set ringing.)

Tynron Doon was well beaten, but when the time of the Montague Dawson race at Southwell was approaching I said to Don that I wanted to watch that race in the racecourse betting shop. 'Don't bother,' he said, 'that horse is completely useless. You'll be wasting your time.' But I insisted that we watch the Southwell race.

Useless Montague Dawson might have been in Don's opinion, but he played his part perfectly that day. Ridden by Steve Drowne, now a top-flight jockey but then a little-known 5-pound claiming apprentice, Montague Dawson took the lead with more than a furlong to go. Watching from Market Rasen, I started jumping up and down and yelling 'Come on, my son! Come on, my son!', much to Don's alarm, and I roared the horse home to win by a length and a quarter.

Don was baffled by my excitement, but I somehow managed to convince him that I just liked the horse and was pleased to see him get his first win.

Not long after that, Norma and Don split up. I hope the Montague Dawson scheme wasn't part of the reason!

Suivez, a horse I co-owned with my friend Ralph Peters, who ran the iced-drink company Slush Puppie in Britain, was also trained by Norma. He started the 1994-5 season with a real bang, winning at Market Rasen and then at Newton Abbot, ridden on both occasions by Norman Williamson – with whom I now work on the BBC jump racing coverage.

Next time out Suivez ran in a handicap hurdle at Stratford-on-Avon, when it took all of Norman's strength to squeeze him home by a short head from Southampton, trained by Ian Balding's brother Toby.

Then the 'ding dong' chimed, and it was announced that Southampton's rider, some seven-pound claiming conditional jockey who had recently come over from Ireland to join Toby, had objected to Suivez. Cheek! Norman was one of the very best jump jockeys around and at the height of his powers – at the Cheltenham Festival that season he won both the Champion Hurdle and the Gold Cup – and this kid had scarcely got off the ferry. In fact he hadn't yet ridden a single winner in Britain.

The objection was kicked out, Suivez kept the race, and only four days later that young lad from Ulster did ride his first British winner. Let me know if you can tell me what happened to him. His name was Anthony Peter McCoy.

Suivez later won two valuable handicap hurdles at Ascot on consecutive Saturdays in 1996, and the same year ran in the Galway Hurdle. He was a hell of a horse.

Then there was Laughing Gas, also co-owned with Ralph and trained by Norma. He ran eighteen times and won only once, but we made sure that the money was down when that moment came, at Fakenham in May 1995.

Ralph would sometimes take a share in my book at a racecourse, which meant that in return for taking on part of the risk, he'd earn a proportion of the profits or stand a proportion of the losses.

One day he told me that he fancied laying a particular horse at Wincanton, so as I was betting somewhere else that day he went down to the Somerset course and ran our pitch there. That evening he phoned me and proudly announced, 'We got it beat, Gal – we got it beat! I told you we'd get it beat.' It was only when I looked in the *Racing Post* the following day that I learned that the horse in question had been twenty lengths clear of the field when falling at the last. Still, getting one beat is getting one beat, whatever the whole story.

Owning racehorses had another benefit for me, beyond the sheer enjoyment of it and the opportunity for the occasional touch like Vado Via at Haydock. It advertised to the outside world that I was a successful man, that I was not short of a bob or two – whether in reality that happened to be true or not.

From the very beginning of my bookmaking career I tried to stick by my one very important rule: if you're down, never ever show it. I could have won two grand or I could have done two grand, but my face would never tell people which it was. If punters thought I was doing well, then they wouldn't have any worries that they'd not be paid by me. Or at least that was the theory.

Even when I was up against it and the money all seemed to be flowing in one direction – away from me, that is – I'd try to give the impression that I was doing well, and I'd always arrive at the racecourse driving some swanky Mercedes, even though

I might not have had enough readies to put petrol in it. If I'd pulled up in an old van the punters would have been put right off, and would have gone off and bet with another bookie.

Making a book on the rails put me in competition with the big firms and the regular independents like Mickey Fletcher, 'The Asparagus Kid' – so called because he used to buy asparagus on the way to the races and sell it or give it to his mates – or Dudley Roberts, with whom I had so many sports bets over the years that I probably still owe him a few quid now. It was through Dudley that I had one of the most memorable – and educational – lunches of my life, with the iconic Irish punter and owner J.P. McManus and Derrick Smith, both of them high rollers closely involved in the Coolmore racing and breeding operation. Dudley took me to lunch with these two legends of the betting ring at a wonderful restaurant named Signor Sassi in Knightsbridge, and just listening to the conversation that day taught me a vast amount about the game.

In the betting ring I needed to attract attention to myself through shouting out the odds louder and – let's not pretend otherwise – by my sheer physical presence. I was just a Cockney spiv up in the Midlands, and needed to make my presence felt – and did so well enough to have the occasional bit of business with another Cockney boy made good – spectacularly good, compared with little old me – in the shape of Michael Tabor, another of the key figures in Coolmore.

In his early days Michael had owned a string of betting shops under the name Arthur Prince, and he was a fearless punter – truly one of the big rollers.

I was betting on the rails one day at Leicester – a dismal, cold, rainy day – and was standing freezing to death and dreaming of a nice big steak and a bottle of red wine when a helicopter came and landed in the centre of the course. Out stepped Michael, who had a very hotly fancied runner in the last race but was intending to dabble in the earlier races.

I hadn't met him before, but that didn't mean that I wasn't happy to take his money on the earlier races. He had some decent bets with me but they all lost – to the point where, with just the last race to come, I was about forty grand up. He clearly expected to win it all back with his hotpot in the last, and since I'd had a strong whisper that his horse would win, I thought: I don't really fancy this.

So I pulled the flaps of my little sign off the rails and made a quick getaway – and heard later that when Michael came out the paddock after seeing his horse out, he was outraged to find that I'd done a runner.

Soon after I'd sent the statement to his home in Monte Carlo he phoned up and gave me a right coating, saying that he'd been going to bet with me, and I shouldn't have ducked out, and I was a disgrace to the bookmaking business, and so on.

I replied that I'd never forget going home from Oxford dogs when I'd done all my money, and trying to get a bet on in one of his Arthur Prince betting shops in Bicester, only to be knocked back. He took it all in good part.

You might think that at the small country tracks there wouldn't be much money to be made by a bookmaker, but you'd be wrong. Plenty of those local farmers were not averse to putting serious money down on one they fancied, and the small rails bookmaker could take much more at Ludlow or Hereford than at some of the biggest meetings. (For the rails minnow, Royal Ascot could be the worst place of all, as few of those posh people in their top hats and tails bothered to weigh themselves down with readies.) From my own point of view, I always felt much more at home on the smaller tracks where you didn't have to be suited and booted, and later on, when I was better known, enjoyed being a big fish in a small pond.

There was a regular punter named Jim Francome – no relation to the great John Francome, so far as I know – whom I called 'Old Man John'. He was from a travelling community, and he liked nothing better than a really big bet.

One Bank Holiday Monday I was betting on the rails at Uttoxeter, and he came up to me before racing and said, 'Gal, I want to have six grand on my horse today. How can I get it on?'

I thought there'd be no problem, then hastily changed my mind when he told me that the horse would be 33-1. No Uttoxeter bookie on a Bank Holiday would take a bet of £6,000 at 33-1, but I made a suggestion: he could get £3,000 on – though little of it would be at 33-1 – if he spread the money around various bookies, and I and my clerk Peter Houghton would try to get the other £3,000 on.

Jim agreed that it was worth a try, so counted out £3,000 for me and Peter, and went off.

When betting on the race opened we were quickly into our

stride, starting at the back row of bookmakers and getting as much on as we dared. The 33-1 didn't last a moment, and the price came tumbling down, until the horse started at something like 2-1.

He duly sluiced in, and after we'd been paid out, Old Man Jim came along to settle up. We'd managed to get our share of his money on at an average of around 10-1, so I handed over £30,000.

'What's this?,' Jim asked in shock.

'Thirty grand – what you won.'

'But the starting price was 2-1,' he said. He'd only got his money on at SP, and hadn't realised that we were backing the horse at the best price we could find at all the lower pitches! He gave us a very decent drink indeed on the strength of what we'd won for him. (By the way, the caravan used by Brad Pitt in the Guy Ritchie film *Snatch*, released in 2000, was Jim's mum's, near Newmarket.)

Of the more prestigious racecourses, Glorious Goodwood has always been a great place to bet, but there I'd prefer to be taking money off the ordinary people in the Silver Ring than the nobs in the Richmond Enclosure.

But when I was starting out at racecourses, unless you'd been able to buy a pitch through the 'dead men's shoes' system then in operation, a small bookmaker could drive all the way to a racecourse, only to find on arrival that there were no pitches free.

That might sound aggravating, but that was how the system worked, and I soon got used to swallowing my disappointment and drowning my sorrows in one of the great variety of eating places to be sampled along the way. Somewhere near every course where I bet there was a favourite restaurant or pub or cake shop, and whether I was up or down or hadn't been able to get a pitch, the driving home would have its positive side.

I was driving over 80,000 miles a year, and sometimes it felt like I was getting through a similar number of calories each day.

On the way to Salisbury racecourse we'd always stop off at a wonderful baker's shop in Amesbury, where we'd load up with rolls and cakes and pies, fuel to keep us going through the afternoon's toil. Believe me, counting your money can be a very tiring business.

Newton Abbot or Devon and Exeter, where in the old days the new jumping season would traditionally begin, always gave the opportunity to eat at The Gissons Arms, which had one of the best restaurants in Devon.

And at Newton Abbot racecourse itself, the speciality was sea food. Just behind the stands, between Tatts and the Silver Ring, there was a fantastic fish stall where they used to sell juicy crab claws, jellied eels that slipped down a real treat, succulent rollmops, and all sorts of other irresistible snacks.

There were plenty of real characters in the West Country betting rings back then – like 'Conky' Lovelace, who along-side his bookmaking was the Town Crier in Yeovil – and Rob Newton, who in addition to betting on the rails had a casino in Torquay. Dodger McCartney was a legend of the ring, while Eddie Baxter made a book under the name Avalon – 'Have it on with Avalon' was the company's slogan.

Bernard Redfern was the father of Anthea, of *Generation*

Game and Bruce Forsyth fame. Another rails bookmaker at Newton Abbot had an even more significant family connection: David Pipe senior, father of Martin, the trainer who changed the whole complexion of the game in the 1990s. When Martin had a runner, you can be sure that we were all taking on board how Dave had priced it up, and made our own prices accordingly. When Dave knew that one of Martin's was the business, you'd have been mad to think different.

Simon Redfern, who was Bernard's nephew, bet further down the rails and was a dead ringer for Freddie Mercury of Queen – and whatever the weather, he wore a long leather overcoat – while Terry Sanders stood a decent bet and had a lovely line in patter with the punters: having agreed a hefty wager, he'd point theatrically to his satchel and sing out, 'Put it in, boy – put it in!'

Brian Wright, who would later attract notoriety as 'The Milkman' in a drugs-related race-fixing scandal, would often come down, stay in the Palace Hotel at Torquay, and take on us bookies at Newton Abbot – which for some reason always felt much more fun than the other racecourse in that area, then known as Devon and Exeter (now just Exeter).

At Goodwood the main bookies' hotel was the Royal at Bognor Regis, which had the added advantage of being regularly frequented by the girls who ran the Tote on the racecourse. During the big Goodwood meeting at the end of July, a night on the town for the Ladies in Red would always end up at the disco at the Royal, and there were a good few tales to be told the following day …

I have to admit that the size of my girth – which some of

you might just have noticed – can be attributed in great part to all the lovely food I'd eat while driving between home and far-flung racecourses. Apart from all those bakeries with the irresistibly lovely smells and fish restaurants where you pick out your lobster and the carveries where you could load your plate with all you could eat – and then some – and those groaning sweet trolleys with profiteroles and apple pie and raspberry flan, I was such a big customer at McDonald's that they should have had a model of me up there with Ronald McDonald.

(By the way, here's a suggestion which has nothing to do with dogs or horses. Whenever you go into a nice restaurant, give the waiters a tip before you start tucking in, rather than afterwards. That way they'll look after you properly straight off.)

Best of all for adding a few inches round the waistline was Ludlow. The route from home to the Shropshire track took me through Kidderminster to Cleobury Mortimer, where there was a great fish and chip restaurant much favoured by the bookmaking fraternity – old-time bookies like Sammy Nixon and Don Butler, who used to bet on the 'away' meetings – and, almost as good, a hotel with a tremendous carvery.

But the real reason why Ludlow is an extra-special racecourse for me is because it was there that in 1994 I met Sue Hogan.

Actually I'd encountered her once before. I'd had a horse running at Wolverhampton and was dining in the wonderful panoramic restaurant there, and I wanted to get my Jackpot bet on, as there was a big carry-over from the previous day and the pool was bigger than usual.

111

The Tote lady who came to our table to take bets was Sue, who had had a flower shop in Birmingham and was now working as a supervisor for the Tote, which that evening was starting to use hand-held terminals for punters to make a bet. She keyed my Jackpot bet into her terminal, I handed over money, and off she went. My first selection got beaten. End of story.

Not quite. It turned out that I hadn't given her the right money, and within a few minutes she came back and said, 'Sorry, but you were £60 short.' I paid up, and off she went again. I often think how different life would have been had I given her the proper money that night.

A few weeks later I met her again. I'd taken a pitch at Ludlow, and on this particular day favourite after favourite was going in and my funds were going down. Only one thing for it: food. So I went off and bought an ice cream, and was leaning against the door of the Tote Credit office having a good old lick, when who should come out and bump straight into me than one of the Tote supervisors that day, none other than that nice lady who'd taken my bet at Wolverhampton?

She later told me that when she clapped eyes on me that day I looked like a tramp, wearing some scruffy jacket and a flea-bitten cloth cap and looking really down in the dumps.

'You look unhappy!', she said to me: 'With all these favourites winning I thought you'd be smiling.' She didn't know I was a bookie, and obviously thought I was a Billy Bunter – a punter.

The following week I was betting on the rails at Worcester when she walked by and saw my stand, and realised that I was a bookmaker – which of course was why I hadn't been smiling when all the jollies were going in at Ludlow.

Then I met her again at Uttoxeter, and we started getting to know each other better. She was married with three children, which made our getting together far from easy, but eventually things got sorted out.

Not long after Sue and I had got together, when everything else was going so well, she came with me to the races at Yarmouth. My pitch there was usually next to that of the late Roy Christie, one of the old brigade of bookies and sadly missed in the betting ring since his death a few years ago.

One day Roy wasn't there, and a local poultry farmer who was one of his usual big punters came up and wanted a bet with me. It was for ten grand, and the horse got beaten.

Next race, he was back with another ten grand – and *that* horse was beaten. Then another ten grand, with the same outcome. I stood every bet, and by the end of the afternoon I was up to the tune of £60,000.

As soon as racing was over we went outside the racecourse, jumped in the nearest cab, and asked the driver to take us up the coast to find somewhere good to eat in one of the local villages. We ended up in a place called Winterton-on-Sea, not far from Yarmouth, and had a great meal in a pub called The Fisherman's Return. Behind the pub was a lovely little house named Harbour Cottage, which as luck would have it was for sale.

I've always loved that area – I long ago decided that my ambition when I finally retire is to make a book at Yarmouth dog track – and it looked like now was the chance to have a place there. So the following morning we went back and bought it for £60,000. (You can look it up in the Hoseasons brochure if you want to know what it looks like now!)

Over the next couple of years we'd go there as often as we could. It was a real haven of peace away from the jungle of the betting ring and the demanding life of driving to a different course every day. I'd like nothing better than to sit out in the garden of a summer evening, sipping quietly at a nice bottle of Chablis while we worked our way through a few crabs from Cromer. That was the life, and I wish we could have spent much more time there than we were able to.

But far too soon, and completely out of the blue, it was taken from us, thanks to a man named Frankie Dettori.

5

'I think I've lost a million quid today'

Isn't it funny how an event which changes your life completely can spring from another event nothing at all to do with you?

On the morning of Saturday 28 September 1996 there was an almighty tailback on the M40 going north from Banbury. I still have no idea why. Perhaps some lorry had shed its load, or someone had had a prang.

Whatever had caused that jam, it set in motion the chain of events which for me ended in disaster. But a disaster which in the long run turned out to be the making of me, as it's no exaggeration to say that without that M40 tailback you would not be reading these words.

As I got in the car that morning, life could hardly have been better. Business was booming, and I had plenty to show for all the hard work which had got me where I was. A few weeks earlier, Sue and I had moved into 'The Winning Post', our five-bedroomed house near Towcester, where side by side in the drive were two Mercedes E320 convertibles. We also had the cottage at Winterton-on-Sea in Norfolk and the villa in Portugal, and I still had my half share in Warren House in Little Horwood.

And Sue and I knew that things were about to get even better, as she was due to have our first baby in just a few weeks' time.

That Saturday was to be simply another working day, the sort of day I loved: betting at the jumps meeting at Worcester racecourse.

In fact my working day had in effect started the night before, when late on Friday evening I'd driven down to King's Cross station in London to pick up the first editions of the *Racing Post* and *Sporting Life* so that I could take a good look at the Saturday cards. That would determine which race meeting I'd go to: Worcester or Ascot.

The Ascot card consisted of seven races, headed by the highly prestigious Queen Elizabeth II Stakes over a mile, which formed the highlight of the Festival of British Racing. This fixture was a showpiece for the Flat game which had understandably attracted some very good horses indeed, as well as all the top jockeys. I vaguely noticed that the reigning champion jockey Frankie Dettori, the irrepressible Italian wonder-boy who by then had made himself wildly popular with racing fans and whose bubbly enthusiasm had breathed such life into the Flat racing scene, had rides in all seven races.

Compared with Ascot, the jumps meeting at Worcester offered much humbler fare. Worcester is a course which rarely hits the racing headlines – except when the nearby River Severn bursts its banks and submerges the course – and that day the racing was pretty moderate. While the Queen Elizabeth II Stakes was worth £199,020 to the winner, the winning owner in the richest race at Worcester would receive a mere £4,922.

I've always felt far more at home at the small jumping meetings than at any of the glamorous days of the Flat, but that was not the only reason why I decided to go to Worcester.

The fact was that the Ascot card looked very tricky from a bookmaker's point of view, while the Worcester programme seemed to offer the opportunity to make some decent money.

When making a book on the horses or the dogs, I've always liked to get stuck into a hot favourite – trying to get those short-priced ones beat, and taking two or three grand out of the race. That simply wouldn't be possible with such a competitive card as Ascot's.

So Worcester it was. I eased myself into the driver's seat of the Merc, and off I set.

That morning's route was simplicity itself: across from Towcester on the A43 to the M40, north on that motorway for a bit, then cut across towards Worcester on the M42.

I was just coming up to the M40 junction at Banbury when – bugger! – I clocked that line of solid, motionless traffic on the northbound carriageway. I pulled into a lay-by just short of the motorway, turned off the engine, and sat and fumed.

Should I keep trying to get to Worcester, or go and work at one of the day's other meetings? The answer was obvious, so I phoned my clerk Peter Houghton, who lived at Swindon and was due to meet me at Worcester, and told him: 'Change of plan – we're going to Ascot.' The Ascot card looked hard, but if we kept playing small and fiddled around we'd probably be going home a few quid up.

I told Peter that I'd see him there, and as I drove down onto the south-bound M40 I felt sorry for the poor sods stuck in the queue going the other way. Had any of us known what was about to happen, they might just have felt sorry for me.

Ascot in those days had some twenty betting pitches on the rails, and when I arrived at the course, as luck would have it there were two free, at the far end furthest down from the stand.

There were some very familiar names among the top rails bookmakers at Ascot: William Hill, Ladbrokes, Corals, Sunderland, Victor Chandler, plus the legendary Stephen Little, the clergyman's son who was fabled for taking a six-figure bet without batting an eyelid.

In such company I was way out of my depth, like a footballer from the Conference playing against the cream of the Premier League, but I could still make an honest day's living.

Peter was already at our lowly rails pitch when I arrived, and together we set up and waited for the action to begin.

The first four races were being televised by the BBC, and at the same time as we were setting up, around the country mug punters in betting shops were filling out slips for fancy multiple bets and accumulators on some of Frankie's seven rides. Some even bet on exotic combinations of all seven, though even the muggest of mug punters knew that in the history of horseracing no jockey had ever won all the races on a seven-race card. Gordon Richards and Alec Russell had both gone through six-race cards long, long ago, and at far humbler meetings, but the idea of any rider winning all seven at such a high-class fixture as Ascot that September Saturday in 1996 was frankly absurd. Frankie was by then a great jockey, but such a feat was beyond even him.

For me and Peter the afternoon began extremely quietly, and for the first race, the Cumberland Lodge Stakes, we took hardly a single bet. Frankie's mount Wall Street, trained by Saeed bin Suroor for the Sheikh Mohammed-inspired Godolphin operation, opened at 5-2 and was backed down to 7-4 before easing a bit and going off the 2-1 'jolly'. He won by half a length from Salmon Ladder.

It was a good start to the afternoon for Frankie fans, but neither here nor there to us.

Business was just as quiet for us on the second race, the Diadem Stakes, one of the top sprints of the season. Lucayan Prince, ridden by Walter Swinburn, was a warm favourite, and further up the rails from us some decent bets were being laid on him: one of £4,000, reported the *Sporting Life* the next day, another of four grand, two of £3,000 and three of £2,000. This was the sort of race with a warm favourite to be opposed in our book, but we were very much the little boys of the betting ring that afternoon, and the serious punters were being accommodated further up, so we continued to play very small.

Frankie was riding Diffident, like Wall Street an inmate of the Godolphin stable, and there seemed very little confidence behind the colt. He started at 12-1, but had a dream run while Lucayan Prince was getting into all sorts of traffic trouble, and Frankie squeezed Diffident home a short head in front of the jolly. Everyone seemed to think that Lucayan Prince had been very unlucky not to have won. The form book was later to describe him as 'the moral victor of this race' but that wasn't much consolation to me. Lucky winner or not, Diffident and Frankie were the winners.

As far as our takings were concerned, things brightened up a little on the run-up to the third, the Queen Elizabeth II Stakes, but we still only took a few hundred quid.

The French colt Ashkalani, owned by the Aga Khan, was favourite, with One Thousand Guineas winner Bosra Sham, ridden by Pat Eddery, and Frankie's mount Mark Of Esteem, another Godolphin colt who had won the Two Thousand Guineas earlier that season, going off joint second favourites at 100-30.

Bosra Sham looked nailed on as she went clear of the others at the furlong pole, but then Frankie, crouched low in the saddle, got an amazing late run from Mark Of Esteem to collar her close home and notch up his third winner.

A Dettori treble was great for the big-race day atmosphere, and fantastic for betting shop punters with their trebles and Patents and Yankees. But for us, minnows on the racecourse, it hadn't affected us at all. We were ahead of the game in a pretty minor way, and I was still wishing I'd managed to get to Worcester, where it would have been a surefire payday.

It was only in the lead-up to the fourth race that I started to feel the beginnings of the adrenaline rush which would soon be pushing me to the very brink of ruin.

This was the Tote Festival Handicap over seven furlongs, a really competitive affair with a big field, and Roger Charlton-trained High Summer a well backed favourite. Frankie was riding Decorated Hero, who had to lug top weight of 9st 13lb and seemed to be facing an enormous task. He'd been available early that morning at 12-1, but with the weight of betting shop liabilities coming into the course market, he opened on course at around 7-1 – the price at which, despite having shrunk to 11-2 for a short while, he started – and won by three and a half lengths.

BBC Television had been scheduled to broadcast the first four races of the afternoon, and it's an indication of how the excitement was building up by now that they decided to keep the coverage going on *Grandstand*, and show the next race live – just in case Lanfranco Dettori increased his tally to a remarkable five.

Still we weren't that affected. By the time of the off for the fifth race we'd been struggling to take more than two grand, and we were roughly £800 up on the day.

In the fifth race, the Rosemary Rated Stakes, Dettori was riding another Godolphin horse: a filly named Fatefully, who in the morning prices had been quoted at around 9-2. But in the Ascot betting ring, where the big firms were trying to limit the damage from Frankie's having ridden the first four winners, she opened at around 5-2 and was solidly backed down to as skinny a price as 13-8.

In an unwitting rehearsal of what was to happen two races

later, I decided that under 2-1 about what had been a 9-2 shot a few hours earlier – and in a field of eighteen runners – was a gift to any right-thinking bookmaker, and laid Fatefully accordingly, taking some reasonably large bets.

Starting at 7-4, she took the lead with just over a furlong to go and, although fiercely challenged by the outsider Abeyr close home, clung on to her advantage and won by a neck.

So Frankie had had five winners so far, one of which had won by a short head and another by a neck. It was looking very much as if God was not on the side of the bookies.

Even with all the bedlam breaking out around us, I had little difficulty keeping my feet on the ground. I fancied Frankie to win the Blue Seal Stakes which was coming up next, and took the decision not to get involved in that at all.

There were only five runners, with Frankie's mount Loch Angel – trained by Ian Balding, father of Clare, whom we last met riding Ross Poldark and with whom I now work for the BBC – 5-4 joint favourite with the Henry Cecil-trained Corsini, who had opened up odds on but whose price had eased as the money came flooding in for Frankie. Further up the rails from us, some very hefty bets were being taken on Frankie's filly, including a £16,000 to win £20,000. But I was happy to stay on the sidelines and not get involved.

Just as well, as Loch Angel won quite cosily by three quarters of a length from Corsini.

Six out of six, and we were only one race away from racing history being made – big time.

The seventh and last race was the Gordon Carter Handicap over two miles, in which Frankie was riding an old gelding named Fujiyama Crest for Newmarket trainer Michael (now Sir Michael) Stoute.

In the morning papers Fujiyama Crest had been priced among the outsiders for the Gordon Carter Handicap, generally at around 12-1 and as long as 20-1 in one place. But as the afternoon progressed and punters around the nation became aware of Frankie's apparently unstoppable surge towards racing history, the betting shops were being landed with ever-growing liabilities through an avalanche of multiple bets on his rides in the later races. It was the best example ever of how the weight of money affects prices. The more that people lumped on, the lower the price of Frankie's horse fell.

Look at this another way: 20-1 meant that the horse was considered to have roughly a 5 per cent chance of winning, while 2-1 meant that he was considered to have a 33 per cent chance. Which, in terms of form and all the rest of it, was closer to reality?

Weight of money didn't make Fujiyama Crest a better horse, or his opposition weaker. Furthermore, he was wearing blinkers, and as both punter and bookmaker I'm always very wary of any horse wearing them. To me, Fujiyama Crest was unreliable, in racing parlance a 'dog' – and laying dogs had long been where I made my living!

If before the avalanche of money he had been anything up to a 20-1 shot, that was a realistic price, and the ones which were showing on the bookies' boards in Tatts or being yelled across an increasingly hysterical Members' Enclosure – 3-1, 11-4, 5-2, 9-4 – were not.

No, those low prices were worse than unrealistic. They were barmy, stark staring bonkers, insane. As far as I was concerned, if Fujiyama Crest had been a 12-1 shot in the morning he was still a 12-1 shot, Frankie Dettori or no Frankie Dettori. Yes, Frankie was on fire by then, but how could that in itself make Fujiyama Crest run faster?

Obviously with everyone around me going 5-2 or lower I'd have been barmy myself to offer anything like that morning price. But here was what appeared a heaven-sent opportunity, a once-in-a-lifetime chance, to lay around 4-1 or 3-1 about a horse whose odds should have been five times that. It was a licence to print money, I thought as I took our first bet: £5,000 at 4-1 from bookmaker Roy Christie.

Then Ralph Leveridge of Coral started firing in bets at us, starting with £40,000 at 7-2, then £20,000 at the same price. The more we took, the more people were scrabbling to get on.

It's important to be clear that none of these bets were in cash, and the great majority were from other bookmakers who were desperately looking to hedge their own liabilities as off-course money flooded into the on-course market. If one of the big chain bookmakers had taken a sizeable bet on Fujiyama Crest at 3-1 and they could back the horse with me at 7-2, clearly that was sound business.

As far as I was concerned, the situation was a licence to print money. Well, almost …

With the big bookies on the rails now going as low as 6-4, as the off-course bookmakers were trying to force the price to odds on to limit their massive liabilities, I was still calling out 3-1, and attracting loads of takers.

It would have taken a machine gun to stop me over the next twenty minutes as Roy Christie was followed by a flood of others, all betting big – some in ten grands, some even six figures. The representatives of the major high-street betting shops were coming in hard, as well as some of the tic-tacs.

I really can't remember those few minutes in any detail. Peter was rushed off his feet, recording in the ledger all the bets that were raining down on us. But I never had the chance to pause and assess how deeply I was going in. It was a maelstrom. It was chaos. But all the while I was thinking: 'At the end of all this I'm going to have half a million pounds wrapped round my bollocks to play with for the rest of my life.'

It was like being on the stage, an end-of-the-pier performance. I was taking the world on. It was my fifteen minutes of fame. There was I, that kid who'd come from selling flowers down Leather Lane market, now at the very centre of things on the greatest racecourse in the world.

I'm not kidding: it felt fantastic.

And it never entered my mind that Fujiyama Crest could win.

At the off I was going 9-4, a fraction longer than Fujiyama Crest's starting price of 2-1 – he got as low as 6-4 before easing half a point – and things only started to calm down once the race had started.

The Gordon Carter Handicap began a little down the straight from the Ascot grandstand, which the runners passed before going out for one whole circuit of the course. As they came past us – with me, at the lowest rank of the rails bookies, very close to the action – the place went wild, and I started to get caught up in the mood. I'd had neither time nor inclination to pause for a second and work out what my liabilities would be in the event – for me, the unthinkably unlikely event – of Fujiyama Crest winning, though I had a vague idea that I'd taken in the region of £500,000.

Frankie and Fujiyama Crest took the lead early on, and as they went past the hysterical stands and down towards Swinley Bottom at the far end of the racecourse, the delirium in the crowd kept scaling fresh heights. Bizarrely, I found myself thinking: I might be teetering on the brink of ruin, but at least I'm witnessing one of the greatest racing moments ever.

Fujiyama Crest held the lead quite cosily all the way round Swinley Bottom, and as the field met the rising ground taking them back towards the straight was still going very easily within himself. He was running more like a 2-1 chance than a 20-1 shot, but still I didn't appreciate the true scale of what was unfolding before me.

At Ascot the long tradition is that they ring a bell as the field swings into the short straight. As I heard it ring out, Fujiyama Crest was still leading.

The cheering was getting louder and louder and louder, and then – thank you, oh thank you, God! – Pat Eddery on a horse named Northern Fleet came out of the pack and started to lay down a serious challenge to Fujiyama Crest. As the two horses

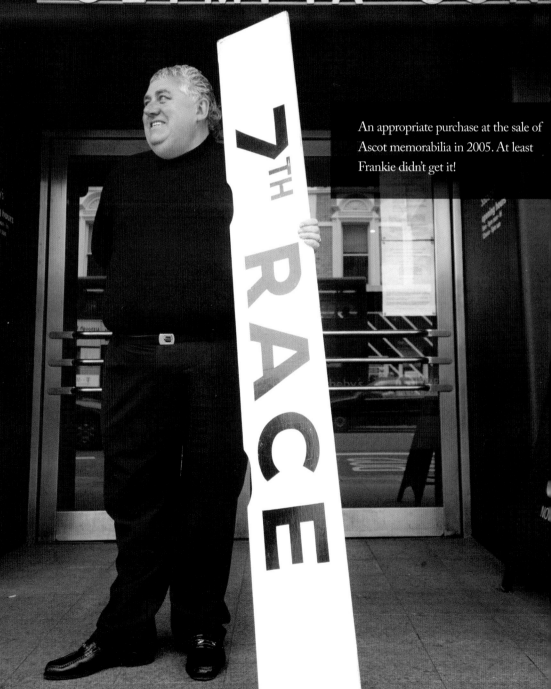

Sotheby's EST.1744

OLYMPIA CON

7TH RACE

An appropriate purchase at the sale of Ascot memorabilia in 2005. At least Frankie didn't get it!

Above: Sue and I on our wedding day. Little did she know what she was letting herself in for …

Below: With my lovely daughter Kelly on her wedding day in June 2006 – but just to show what a great father I was, I left before the end of the reception as I was covering the Greyhound Derby final on Sky!

Son Charlie paying his respects to Coral, whose understanding after Dettori Day really saved my bacon.

The Mi Odds touch at Hereford in March 2002. *Above*: David Dennis takes him to post, and *below*, David with Sue and me in the winner's enclosure.

Above: Cheer up, Norma – we've won again! Sharing a joke with my trainer …

Below: Charlie and me on the right after Offshore Fox had won at Harlow in 2009, with my first putter-on Chris Barker third from the left.

At the John Lovell Betting Exchange Office in Cardiff. *Above*: Brett Lloyd with one of the fruits of his labours. *Below*: Gal gets down among the clever boys.

Partners in pleasure. *Above*, going to the dogs with Dave Smith for Sky, and *below*, with John Parrott at Aintree for the Beeb.

Happy family in Lanzarote: *left to right*, Faye, Gal, Sue, Charlie and Liam.

came past me it looked as if I might yet be spared ruin, but it was as if the stands themselves, as well as every single person in them, were willing on Frankie and Fujiyama Crest, and that old dog managed to keep his blinkered head in front and hold off Northern Fleet to win by a neck. A neck!

Total bedlam, and it's very hard to explain how I felt as Frankie went past the post in front. A combination of horror and a weird sort of elation, as I'd just seen a unbeatable moment of racing history.

Then I saw Peter staring into space, looking completely shell-shocked, all the colour drained from his face. I punched him hard on the arm – even money he still has the bruise now – to bring him round.

There was chaos in the winner's enclosure, with Frankie being cheered and cheered, and repaying the acclamation by spray-ing the crowd with champagne. But Peter and I couldn't hang around to watch all that.

As quickly as we could we made our way to Car Park 3 so that we could assess the damage in comparative peace. We got into my car and started going down the ledger in more detail, and as I ran my finger down the rows of recorded bets an icy trickle ran down my neck as I thought to myself: Fuck me, I could be in trouble here.

That was the understatement to end all understatements. I was scarcely halfway down the ledger when it became clear just how bad the damage was, and the name of one firm was point-ing at me, like the rifles of a firing squad:

Coral	£40,000 at 7-2
Coral	£20,000 at 7-2
Coral	£30,000 at 3-1
Coral	£10,000 at 3-1
Coral	£40,000 at 11-4
Coral	£10,000 at 5-2
Coral	£10,000 at 9-4

I'll save you the bother of doing the sum. I owed Coral alone £487,500 – nearly half a million smackers.

And all told the total was over a million pounds. Over a million pounds …

I was in a daze, but had to pull myself together, as my working day was very far from over. Earlier that Saturday, when I thought I was going off to win a few quid at the humdrum meeting at Worcester, I'd told my oldest son Nicky that I'd be joining him at Milton Keynes dogs later to run a book on the evening's programme. Nicky had been helping me out for several years, and I knew he could easily hold his own at the pitch until I got there.

Peter got out of the Merc and walked ever so slowly back to his own car, still in a state of shock and trying to come to terms with what he'd just been part of, while I took a large dose of the only medicine I had handy, Chas and Dave blaring out of the speakers more loudly than ever. I just had to drown the whoops of delight and appreciation which I could still hear a hundred yards away in the winner's enclosure.

I drove away from Ascot racecourse and made round the M25 and onto the M40, as I'd decided to drop in on my old friend Ralph Peters, who lived in Beaconsfield. As I mentioned earlier, Ralph sometimes took a share in my betting, but had declined to go with me to Worcester as it was too far for his liking that day, and as I never got round to telling him that I'd switched to Ascot, he was not sharing my gains or losses there.

I think he must have been the luckiest man in the world that day, but of course he was not aware of that when he opened the door to me and asked me innocently, 'How did it go today, son?'

I had to tell him straight: 'Ralph, I think I've lost a million quid today.'

To his eternal credit, he made no immediate reaction, but sat me down with a stiff drink and went off into his kitchen. Three minutes later he emerged with a plateful of smoked salmon sandwiches, which were by a long, long way the most delicious smoked salmon sandwiches I've ever tasted – though I couldn't be sure whether the liquid glistening on the top was lemon juice or the tears I was shedding.

I'd promised Nicky that I'd join him at Milton Keynes dogs and, whatever had happened, did not want to let him down. So I drove straight from Ralph's to the dog track, where one race had already been run. Nicky met me with a long face.

'We've had a bad start, Dad,' he said gloomily. 'We've lost seventeen quid on the first.' This put my own day into some sort of perspective, but I didn't yet tell him what had happened.

I took over for the second race, and the first bet I took was from a punter who wanted £1 on a 2-1 shot.

It's going to be a long way back from here, I thought.

6

'It will take time'

Betting with Nicky through the rest of the evening at Milton Keynes dogs kept me from succumbing completely to the shock that had enveloped me at Ascot, but once the last race had been run and he had gone home – I still hadn't told him what had happened – that's when the true scale of the disaster really began to sink in.

Rather than go back to Towcester there and then and confess all to Sue, I drove off from the dog track and found a reasonably secluded lay-by, where I parked up and thought that I'd try to get a few hours' sleep. It had been an incredibly stressful day, and after a while I found myself dropping off – and far from convinced whether or not I wanted to wake up.

I had bouts of fitful sleep, and early the next morning phoned home. There was no reply. That was strange, but I'd have to put off telling Sue for even longer, as I was due to make a book again at Ascot that day, and however stupid I'd been in getting carried away before Frankie's fateful seventh race, I was not about to chicken out or run away and hide.

So after dropping in to a motorway service station to freshen up as best I could, I continued south towards Ascot. Down the

M1, round the M25 and out on the M4, then turning off past Windsor racecourse, and through Windsor Great Park to that first glimpse of the stands – I have to say that the chill I felt that Sunday morning as I got closer and closer to the track is repeated every time I go there, even fifteen years after the event. I don't think that feeling of dread will ever go away.

I parked up and to strike the right note put on a black tie, which I happened to have in the car. Then I went in to meet Peter at our rails pitch. Naturally enough, the place was still buzzing over what had happened there the day before, and while I was not quite the centre of attention, I was in great demand as the personification of a bookmaker who had done his bollocks on the great day.

Loads of other bookies had been very severely hit by Frankie's Magnificent Seven – some were to go out of business because of it – but I was a natural target for the media spotlight: The Bookie who Lost a Million.

First off I was interviewed by a bevy of journalists about exactly what I'd lost. Then I spoke to Sue Barker for BBC television, and she asked me what I'd do if Frankie repeated the feat that day. I said I'd go straight down to Swinley Bottom, at the far end of Ascot racecourse, and drown myself in the reservoir there.

Of course, this was all trying to put on a brave face – and boy did I need a brave face that day. As I walked down the rails to take up the same position as the day before, I could feel the hostility of some – not all – of the other bookies. It was just assumed that I'd been cleaned out several times over and that I'd never be able to pay up, and the same suspicion had obviously got to the punters.

I didn't take a penny on the first race. Nor on the second. Nor on the third. To me it was perfectly clear why the other bookmakers, tic-tacs and punters were steering well clear of me. The word was: Don't bet with Wiltshire; after what happened yesterday, he won't pay.

I was a pariah, an untouchable, and while it made me feel wretched and close to despair, I could see perfectly well why they were thinking that way.

After the third race I decided to give the afternoon up as a bad job and told Peter that there was no point in hanging around for more inactivity. I removed my sign from the rails and made my way back to the car park, where I took off the black tie, turned up the volume on Chas and Dave to even more decibels than the previous day, and drove off. As far as I was concerned at that moment, I would never ever go to Ascot again.

When I reached our house in Towcester, there was no sign of either Sue or her children Liam and Faye, who were living there with us at the time. (Her oldest child Mark had left home.) So I phoned around, and eventually tracked her down to her mother's house in Birmingham, where she'd fled the previous evening.

Sue had not been watching the racing from Ascot on the Saturday afternoon, and had first heard about the Dettori seven-timer on the evening news. But as far as she was concerned that had nothing to do with me, as she knew that I'd gone to Worcester, not Ascot. I hadn't thought to tell her of the change of plan, as on the Saturday morning I had not thought it of great significance.

It was only when a journalist from a local paper rang the doorbell and asked what her reaction was to her husband losing all that money at Ascot that she had the first inkling that something very unusual – and very serious – had happened. You can see why she felt completely at sea. So far as she knew, I'd been at a minor meeting at Worcester, and the next thing she knew I was apparently headline news.

She'd tried to call me on my mobile phone but I had it switched off, so she spent the night not knowing what had become of me – and when she woke to find the house being doorstepped by a horde of other journalists who wanted to fire questions at her about how her partner had blown a million quid thanks to Frankie Dettori, she knew that it was time to get away. So she loaded the two children into the car and drove off to her mother's house near Birmingham.

On the Sunday evening she drove back to Towcester, leaving the children with her mother. The press had drifted away, and we sat down and started to take stock.

There were two options, both pretty stark.

I could declare that I was unable to pay and lose my bookmaker's licence and be 'warned off' racecourses for five years, and then, if I had the stomach for it, could possibly think about starting again. Betting debts were not recoverable at law, so I could wriggle out that way. Professional suicide, as the stigma from not paying up for Dettori Day would never go away, but one hell of a lot less expensive than the other option, that of asking my creditors for time and paying off every penny just as soon as I could.

We needed to calculate what we would raise from selling our worldly goods, and we agreed that, just as soon as we could, we'd go off somewhere quiet and work through what we could do. But no matter how long it took, somehow we would pay everybody we owed.

It's amazing, but I didn't completely lose my sense of humour in the middle of all this disaster. Among the people to whom I now owed large sums of money was Rocky Roberto, a race-course tic-tac from Ilford.

I phoned him, and when he answered I put on a very deep voice and said I was calling from the main police station in Milton Keynes. The body of a very fat person had been found floating lifeless in a lake, I said, and Rocky's business card had been found in his pocket. Did he have any idea who this might be?

Good old Rocky was profoundly shocked, and immediately told them that it must be that overweight bookie Gary Wilt-shire, who'd lost all his money on account of Frankie Dettori and was completely ruined. I didn't string him along for more than a couple of minutes before coming clean that it was me playing a silly joke on him, but I was touched that he was much more concerned by the idea that I'd topped myself than he was by the prospect of not getting his money back!

139

It was one thing to be so determined that everyone would be paid. It was quite another to get each of them to agree a timetable for that, and I knew that before I did anything else, I had to get them all to agree to be paid just as soon as I could manage it.

Top of the list, by a long way, was Coral Bookmakers.

Before dawn on the Monday morning I got up and drove south, stopping on the way to buy that day's *Sporting Life* and *Racing Post*. In 1996 neither paper was published on a Sunday, so Monday was their first chance to report the sensational happenings on Saturday 28 September, and to publish the accounts of that incredible day from those most deeply affected – among them, naturally enough, Gal Wiltshire.

This is what Bob Harman write in the *Sporting Life* under the headline, 'Bold Wiltshire Rues "Chance of a Lifetime"':

> *Gary Wiltshire, the independent rails bookmaker who took on the Ascot ring almost single-handedly in the exchanges leading up to Saturday's final race, yesterday admitted that he had taken 'a real hammering'.*
>
> *Race by race, the Dettori 'magnificent seven' turned into the ultimate layer's nightmare.*
>
> *Minutes before Frankie delivered his coup de grace on Fujiyama Crest, the larger-than-life Wiltshire had taken a bold stand and laid the Michael Stoute-trained gelding to all comers.*
>
> *He estimated that he would clear his mounting losses in one fell swoop.*

Wiltshire, putting a brave face on things yesterday, said: 'Sure, I'm a gambler, but I can assure you that I didn't go there yesterday intending to lay the level of bets that I did, particularly in the last race.

'That was one of the best opportunities to lay a bet that anyone could ever have had in their lifetime – 2-1 being offered about a 12-1 chance was a silly price, but it went and won.'

Wiltshire was loath to discuss his full liabilities for the day, but he revealed: 'I took a £70,000 to £20,000 early on about Fujiyama Crest but that was only the tip of the iceberg. Unfortunately, it did not stop there.

'If the race had been run at ten o'clock this morning, I would still have been there all night trying to lay it!

'But when you are a gambler, you have to gamble – it's a bit like feeding a drug habit. You would like to think that you would never do it again, but you would!'

Reflecting on what started as a pretty innocuous day, Wiltshire added: 'I only took £600 on the first race and won £200, but after Dettori had bagged the first four I was laying substantial amounts on Fatefully in the fifth race, thinking that the 7-4 generally on offer was also a crazy price.

'Usually, my maximum would be around the £4,000 mark, but you get hotted up and get caught in it all.

'To put the whole day in perspective in betting terms, a bookie pal of mine who works down in the Silver Ring even managed to lose £10,000, which must be unheard of.'

He added: 'There must be hundreds of bookmakers throughout Britain who will be hard pushed to keep going after Saturday.

'Needless to say, I didn't stop for an Italian meal on the way home yesterday. I decided to settle for fish and chips!'

The bit about fish and chips instead of an Italian meal was of course a little white lie – me keeping up the act of the jolly Jack the Lad, the Cheeky Cockney. The reality had been that on the Saturday evening the most I'd been able to manage to eat was that smoked salmon sandwich at Ralph's.

And of course it wasn't only in the racing press that the Dettori story made big headlines – and I was wheeled out as one of the day's big losers. Monday's *Daily Express*, for example, quoted me as saying, 'It was the worst day I have ever had. I have never experienced anything like it.' Amen to that!

That Monday morning I felt even worse than I had on Saturday and Sunday, but I was in no doubt about what I had to do: go to the Coral offices in Barking.

Obviously I needed a bit of time to pay their debt, and I knew that the only thing to do was go down at the earliest opportunity and throw myself on the mercy of their top man, Trevor Beaumont.

Trevor has never been in the slightest way high and mighty about his senior position in the bookmaking business, but none the less I was a bit taken aback when, having arrived at the Coral offices in Essex at sparrow's fart, I rang the bell at the main entrance, and the door was opened by … Trevor himself!

'Hallo, Gary,' he said cheerfully as he let me in, 'I can't tell you how good it is to see you!' – and he remained cheerful as I came clean that I didn't have the money to pay Coral, but as soon as I got it, I would be settling every penny of the debt.

'You'll get paid,' I promised him, 'but it will take time.'

Talk about finding out at times like that who your real friends are. Trevor was magnificent. 'You've got a good name,' he said, 'and if you say you'll pay, then I know you will.'

He then told me that he had an emergency meeting with his board of directors later that day, and he'd stick up for me.

But he also told me that the top people from the other major High Street bookies had already been on to him to discuss the position, and the others were all for getting me banned from racecourses. It was their big chance to wipe me out, and they were inclined to take it.

They wanted to squeeze the last drop of blood out of me – and one company, to whom I owed a comparatively small amount, had already been on to me, demanding that their debt was paid within seven days.

Others, notably the main bookmaking organisations in the form of the Betting Office Licensees' Association and the Bookmakers' Protection Association, were complaining vociferously that I had cost them a fortune, as had I not stood against the crowd, the starting price of Fujiyama Crest would have been around evens, which would have saved the other bookies millions.

Warwick Bartlett of the British Betting Office Association told the journalist Brian Radford in the *Sun*: 'If Gary Wiltshire hadn't kept knocking the last winner out, when it should have been shortened, it would have ended up evens, not 2-1. That made a colossal difference and slaughtered my members. He's cost the industry £10 million.'

That was rubbish. As were those stories put about by pathetic rumour-mongers that the seventh race that day had been fixed by the other jockeys to allow Frankie his unique achievement. I was never going to hide behind such stupid suggestions. I knew exactly what had happened, catastrophic as it was for me, and was always going to take my punishment fair and square.

Trevor Beaumont, bless him, earned my eternal gratitude by not going along with those people who wanted my blood and he, more than anyone, saved the situation.

More than anyone except Sue, that is. She was a complete rock – and she was seven months pregnant at the time, with things on her mind much more urgent than sorting out her washed-up husband. She summed up our situation brilliantly: 'One day you're wondering what shade of curtains to put up in the new baby's bedroom. The next day you haven't got a bedroom to put them up in.'

The first thing was to get right away from anywhere we might be tracked down by the media. As soon as I arrived back in Towcester after my meeting in Barking with Trevor Beaumont, we threw a few things into a suitcase, got into the car, and set off.

We went the short distance to the M1, headed north, and drove and drove, with no idea where we were going. It was dusk when we reached Northumberland, dark by the time we crossed the border into Scotland, and still I drove on, probably subconsciously avoiding stopping, as once we stopped, then we'd have to face the extreme discomfort of tackling the situation head on.

It was late in the evening when we reached Loch Lomond, where near the lake we booked into a B&B for the night.

Over the next few days Sue and I walked round and round Loch Lomond talking about what we had to do, and I have to admit that for much of that time I was strongly of the opinion that the simplest way out was for me to belly-flop into the water and have done with it. It was even money whether I wanted to live or die.

Sometimes it's the less than obvious things which push you in the right direction, and I got a big boost on the Tuesday morning when we picked up a *Sporting Life* in a local paper shop – and there was the weekly column by the late Sir Clement Freud. I knew Sir Clement a bit from bumping into him at point-to-points, where his brother Stephen was a regular racegoer as well as being a very keen and clever student of the form book, and always loved his columns. I loved this one in particular for a couple of paragraphs early on:

> *There are jockeys who, when on a high, cause all around*
> *them to hope for their comeuppance. Not on Saturday:*
> *Dettori had 20,000 racegoers and millions more in betting*

shops wanting him to make three successive winners into four, then into five, after that six and the staggering sum of £900,000 in major bets was on him to drive what Time-form called 'a fairly useful handicapper, sometimes wanders in closing stages' to victory in the seventh.

Sincere compliments to Gary Wiltshire, who realised that a natural 12–1 shot whom people want to back at 2s is a proper vehicle for laying; he has my sympathy for losing a lorra cash, though he certainly recouped some on Sunday…

Apart from that last bit about my having got some back on Sunday being well short of the mark, what Sir Clement wrote was spot on: Fujiyama Crest had indeed been 'a proper vehicle for laying'.

I was encouraged to learn that not everyone thought I'd been a complete idiot at Ascot, but expressions of sympathy would not pay off the debts, so as soon as Sue and I were back in Towcester later in the week, we started to try and wipe the slate clean.

The most urgent debt to be cleared was the comparatively small amount owed to another of the major bookmakers, who unlike Trevor Beaumont at Coral were in no mind to help me out in my moment of crisis.

So I had to raise some money double quick. My jewellery was down to the pawnbroker's shop in a flash. Next for the chop were the two Mercs, the great symbols of my success.

By the middle of the week there were no flash cars standing on the drive in front of our house, but by the end of the same week this debt had been paid.

One off the list.

My 'tank' of funds was soon used up paying off the tic-tacs to whom I owed money – none of whom, by the way, ever asked me for it, so trusting were they – and then we had to concentrate on making bigger money from selling the houses.

Warren House at Little Horwood was sold for £635,000 – though I got only half of that, as it was joint-owned with Jackie – and the cottage at Winterton-on-Sea soon went as well, for a joke price of £70,000. The villa in Portugal also went for well under the odds – a really ridiculous price, but I was in no position to complain. I needed the money, and I needed it prontissimo.

Worst of all, the Winning Post at Towcester, of which we were both so proud and which was house and home to us and to Sue's children, had to go as well. We'd only bought it in July 1996, and having to move out in January 1997 was a massive wrench.

With most of the big assets paid off over a year or so after Dettori Day, we still had plenty of lesser debts to square, and to raise a few quid I turned my hand to anything, including another spell selling Christmas paper in Hoe Street market.

And I worked on Sundays at Finmere Market, selling whatever I could lay my hands on.

But there were occasional shafts of light coming through the dark gloom of the tunnel and we tried to make our way forwards. Best of all was the birth of Charlie in December 1996.

And week after week there were little expressions of support, some private and some public, which kept us optimistic that at the end of the day, we'd come out the other side – including a piece by Alastair Down in the *Sporting Life* which so affected me that I still have it framed and hung on the wall in our hall:

> *A jockey rides seven winners in a day only about every 10,000 years, and it was just careless of Gary to be around at the same time …*
>
> *Gary is still about the place, head held high, but he faces years back at the betting coalface with a pick in one hand and a list of people to pay in the other.*
>
> *But at least he is buckling down to it, chiselling a grand here and there and economising as necessary. For example, he is not sending Frankie a Christmas card this year.*

Too right I wasn't!

7

'I think the game's gone'

Rather than be paralysed by the sheer scale of what we had to pay, we concentrated on settling individual debts, and as each one was paid, so a little bit more weight was lifted from our shoulders.

With the Winning Post in Towcester disposed of, we had to find somewhere to live. Sue still had her house in Hollywood, a village between the M42 and the centre of Birmingham. She had been in the process of selling it, but Fujiyama Crest changed all that. It was not a large house, and with two of her children still at home and another one on the way – not to mention my not exactly undersized self – space was extremely limited. So we converted the garage and made it into a bedroom. This was some comedown – from a superb detached house to living in a converted garage.

To be honest, I didn't really care where I lived, so long as I could have a bet, but there were the children and other people to consider, and I was blessed to have Sue at my side as I tried to rebuild my life.

I can't recall the precise moment when we knew that all the debts had been paid, but they were, and I know that through the whole nightmare it was Sue who kept me going. She still does.

The first priority had been to sell the things which could most easily be converted into cash, and the racehorses I owned fitted naturally enough into that category. Off they went – all except one.

Soon after Dettori Day, Sue went to a fortune teller, who looked into her crystal ball and said: 'I see a young horse. Whatever else you do, you must keep this horse.'

Sue did not have to ask which young horse this was. Since Vado Via had stopped racing, she had been boarding at the Manor House Stud, near Tring in Buckinghamshire, and I'd decided to breed from her. Her first foal was a colt, born in mid-June 1996, just three months before Dettori Day.

We named the youngster Mi Odds, in fond memory of my number plate. One evening I had just started my drive home from Epsom races when I was pulled over by a traffic cop on a motorbike. I thought he might be a punter and tried to charm him by asking, 'Have you had a bad evening at Epsom as well?', but he gave me that 'Don't take the piss, son' look, and I knew he wouldn't be humoured.

What he wanted was to point out to me that it was illegal to fiddle around with the spacing in a number plate, and since my plates reading MI ODDS had been made by moving the space in M10 DDS, he was going to phone my local police station, and I'd have to report there the following day with the plates, front and back, restored to their correct form. I did as he asked, but the episode rather spoiled the joke, so when I had an offer of £5,000 for the plates from an Essex bookmaker, I didn't hesitate to add another five grand to the Dettori Day Fund. (My number plate nowadays is GAL 74.)

The equine Mi Odds turned out to be a lovely horse who would win many races for us, none more memorable than a lowly selling hurdle at Hereford in March 2002.

Mi Odds had first gone into training with Norma Macauley, and he did not race until he was a four-year-old in February 2000. He came third at Southwell, and after a few more outings returned there in December 2000 and recorded his first win, and just four days later won again at Wolverhampton.

He won his third race in January 2001 and won again the following month, then seemed to hit a flat spot through the rest of that spring and summer. After he'd finished unplaced at Leicester in July 2001, we gave him a rest.

Norma was essentially a Flat trainer and we thought we could go for a nice touch over the sticks. So early in 2002 I sent Mi Odds to Ian Williams, who trained in Portway, right by where we were then living, and identified what looked like a weak selling race at Hereford in March as the ideal opportunity for his hurdling debut.

I'd seen him burn up the Ian Williams gallops in the weeks before the race, and school brilliantly over the hurdles, so as far as I was concerned he was a stone bonking certainty.

There were sixteen runners in the Hereford-Racecourse.co.uk Novices' Selling Hurdle over two miles and a furlong and, despite the fact that he had not run for seven months, Mi Odds was not unfancied. He opened in the betting ring at around 5-1 and in we steamed, backing him off the boards to the extent that he went off 9-4 joint-favourite with one of Nigel Tinkler's.

We'd impressed upon his jockey David Dennis that the horse needed to be held up and make his challenge as late as possible, so we were alarmed to see Mi Odds pulling like mad in the early stages of the race. David just about managed to anchor him until, with three hurdles to jump, he started to make up ground on the leaders. But when he blundered at the third-last, and again at the second-last, it felt like the longest two-mile hurdle I'd ever witnessed, as he looked bound to get beaten.

Just when I thought our nicely planned coup had flown out the window, he found a fresh wind, took the lead before the last and lasted home to win by a length and a quarter. The comment in the official form book *Raceform* read: 'Mi Odds, a prolific winner on Fibresand, landed a touch for his bookmaker owner on this hurdling debut.' Too right he did!

It had been an amazing training performance by Ian Williams to get Mi Odds ready for the race and we all copped a good few quid – but watching it had not done my heart much good.

As the winner of a selling race, Mi Odds was then immediately offered for sale at the post-race auction. The racecourse auction-eer Jon Williams worked very hard to sell him, but for whatever reason – perhaps it was the looming presence of the bulky owner standing just behind Jon! – there was no bid. Just as well for me, as I'd have gone to at least twenty grand to keep him.

To the best of my recollection Mi Odds did not run over hurdles again. But in all he won fifteen races – thirteen on the all-weather and one on turf on the Flat in addition to the Hereford hurdle race – and gave us a huge amount of pleasure. He was once ante-post favourite for the Winter Derby at Lingfield, and I was offered a six-figure sum for him by some people who thought he'd be an ideal horse to race in the USA. I declined the offer, as he meant so much to me and I wanted to keep him close by.

I could well have done with a few more nags like him.

And I could have done without a few of the big winners who belonged to other people and proved big losers for me in the betting ring. In addition to Fujiyama Crest, a select few stick in the mind.

There was Blowing Wind in the Vincent O'Brien County Handicap Hurdle in 1998, the last race of that year's Cheltenham Festival. In those days the Festival was still over three days and over the meeting I'd done my proverbials. On the first day, Tuesday, the great Istabraq had been 3-1 favourite when winning the first of his three Champion Hurdles and then the hotly fancied Martin Pipe-trained Unsinkable Boxer had won the last, a twenty-four runner handicap, as 5-2 favourite.

That was just the sort of race where I liked to take the favourite on, and I was suitably punished.

Wednesday started badly with favourite French Holly turning in a brilliant performance to win the Royal & SunAlliance Novices' Hurdle and another favourite obliged when Florida Pearl landed the Royal & SunAlliance Chase.

Thursday provided some relief when 25-1 outsider Cool Dawn won the Gold Cup, usually a very strong betting heat, but I was still licking my wounds as the end of the meeting approached – and they took some more vigorous licking when Martin Pipe's well-backed favourite Cyfor Malta landed the penultimate race, the Cathcart.

Like Unsinkable Boxer and Cyfor Malta, Blowing Wind was ridden by Martin Pipe's then stable jockey, the incomparable A.P. McCoy, but as I looked at it, there was every reason to oppose him in the County Hurdle.

For one thing, there were twenty-seven runners for what is always one of the most competitive races of the jumping season.

For another, Blowing Wind had run only five days earlier, when he had won the Imperial Cup at Sandown Park. There was a £50,000 bonus for winning both races, but surely he couldn't be at his peak so soon after another hotly contested race.

On the other hand, Blowing Wind would have been 4lb worse off with his rivals had the handicapper been able to re-rate him after the Sandown race and in the betting ring before the County Hurdle he was coming in for a huge amount of support, with comparatively little interest in any of the other twenty-six runners.

This was not exactly a repeat of Fujiyama Crest, but as far as I was concerned the same principle applied: for a variety of reasons, the horse seemed to have a far worse chance than his odds suggested and therefore he was a horse to lay.

In the ring Blowing Wind was being backed and backed and backed but I stood firm, going 5-2 while all around me the 2-1 was being snapped up. As with Fujiyama Crest, this was simply too good a chance to miss.

And what happened? Do you really have to ask? Blowing Wind started 15-8 favourite, with the second favourite out at 9-1, and under a vintage McCoy drive clawed his way up the hill and won by a length and three-quarters.

McCoy and Pipe were the guv'nors that day all right – and for me it was a very long way home.

The Cheltenham produces a betting-ring buzz like no other, an atmosphere well caught before the first race on the opening day of the 2000 Festival by David Ashforth of the *Racing Post*:

> *Gary Wiltshire will be gutted. Half-gutted. He may be completely gutted later, depending on Flagship Uberalles. Wiltshire's betting in the second row, you can't miss him, big bloke, smiles a lot – at least, he used to, until Monsignor arrived at the winning post before all the others.*
>
> *'What's your plan, Gary?' 'To get Monsignor beaten, and a nice bottle of Chablis tonight, please God.' That's the trouble with God. Sometimes, he passes all understanding, a bit like the Coral Cup.*
>
> *Gary's got one of those 'Specials' on his board, the kind you know should be avoided, but your maths isn't quite good enough to know why: 5-2 the double, Monsignor and Flagship Uberalles.*
>
> *I'm worried for Wiltshire but, then, I used to be worried for Yorkshire, too, when they wouldn't let anyone play for them unless they'd been born there. Granted, Yorkshire was bigger, but not much.*

At the 2002 Festival I got it all wrong again – and this time on the first race of the meeting rather than the last. But I so nearly got it right.

This was just four days after we'd landed that lovely touch with Mi Odds at Hereford. I was very flush with funds, and itching to play them up by taking on a hot favourite at the Festival. There was no better opportunity than in the very first race of the meeting, the Gerrard Supreme Novices' Hurdle.

The hot favourite was Like-A-Butterfly, a mare owned by J.P. McManus and trained in Ireland by Christy Roche, and you did not have to be a genius to see why she was the Irish banker that day. She was unbeaten, having won three bumpers – flat races for jumping horses – and four novice hurdles, and it was an open secret that her owner, a punter of legendary proportions, was keen on her chance that day.

The 2001 Cheltenham Festival had been cancelled on account of the epidemic of foot and mouth disease, so there was an extra dimension to the excitement in the betting ring on that first day of the 2002 fixture, and perhaps that atmosphere got to me, a bit like the atmosphere on Dettori Day.

Whatever the reason, I thought that anything around 2-1 about the jolly in such a keenly contested heat was way too short, and I was determined to get Like-A-Butterfly beat. So, as with Blowing Wind, I stood firm against the favourite. I laid her heavy at my pitch on the lower rails but that wasn't enough for me, so I went up to our pitch in the main ring, where Sue and Peter Houghton were betting at our stand, and laid her some more.

Like-A-Butterfly went off at the ridiculous price of 7-4, but as the runners turned for home and faced towards the final hurdle I was getting a very different feeling from the one I'd had four years earlier. This time I was clearly going to be proved right.

The mare had taken the lead at the second-last hurdle, but in the straight had been joined by another Irish challenger, the Willie Mullins-trained Adamant Approach, ridden by Ruby Walsh. They went to the last neck and neck, but Adamant Approach was clearly going the better. Oh what a lovely start to the year's biggest betting meeting! – and then Adamant Approach mis-timed his take-off and crashed to the ground on landing. Even then Like-A-Butterfly won by only a neck from Westender.

Not for the first time in my life, at a moment of crisis I did a bunk. Leaving Sue and Peter to run the pitch, I just left the racecourse and walked down into the centre of Cheltenham, as if trying to make some contact with the real world after the bedlam of the racecourse. I walked round for something like three hours, then went back up to Prestbury Park when the racing was over to help Peter and Sue pack up.

They were in remarkably chipper mood, since so far as they knew they had managed to recover from the setback with Like-A-Butterfly and had ended the day up after all.

The thing was, they didn't know about the forty grand I'd stood her for on the rails . . .

Oxford dog track was a far cry from the Cheltenham Festival, but for many years it had been a very important part of my working life – not least when a little black bitch named Perbri was going into the traps. Owned by my good pal John Gaisford of the *Oxford Mail*, she was a cute little dog who ran her heart out, but she had one little quirk which I was able to turn to a good profit. She loved to chase the other dogs, but didn't like running past them. So over the years we made good money laying her to our heart's content.

I'd had such fun at Oxford, and it really hurt when in July 2000 I decided to give up my pitch there.

By then I was primarily a racecourse bookmaker. Following the initial shock of losing all that money, and the slog of settling down to pay it off, Dettori Day had done me no harm whatsoever in terms of my public profile. After Barry Dennis, whose slots on Channel 4 Racing had made him a very popular figure for racing fans, I was possibly the most familiar racecourse bookmaker in the country, and with the business going along very nicely I simply had too intense a workload to justify staying at Oxford.

I'd continue to bet at Milton Keynes, which was much closer to home, but something had to give, and that was the Oxford pitch.

But in early January 2001 the greyhound section of the *Racing Post* carried this:

> *Gary Wiltshire is to return to the betting ring at Oxford after an absence of just over six months having admitted it was a 'wrench' to leave in the first place.*

'I said that at the time, but it's been like having my toast without butter since I left,' said Wiltshire. 'I was there twelve years first time around and I suppose it's where I made my name. The only difference now is that I'll be betting as number four having left at number one.

'But I've always thought that a pitch was only as good as the bookmaker there, so I can hopefully build things up quite quickly when I start back . . .'

So back I went.

Just over a year later, in February 2002, the *Post* had another story about me, under the headline, 'Wiltshire to Set Up New Betting Exchange':

Gary Wiltshire, one of Britain's best known on-course bookmakers, is to launch an internet betting exchange on Friday.

The arrival of www.garywiltshire.com, where punters will be able to take and lay bets at their nominated prices, signals an important change of emphasis for its ebullient founder, who from now on plans to stand only at major race meetings and says that betting exchanges have 'seriously affected' on-course business.

Wiltshire's operation coincides with the launch of Betdaq Racing, a UK-based website dedicated to horseracing and backed by Irish financier Dermot Desmond, and presents Betfair, the runaway market leader, with a second new competitor.

Wiltshire aims to price up every horse by 9am each day and will lay bets at both fractional and decimal odds. Commission is on a sliding scale of between one per cent and five per cent, depending on turnover.

'We will be betting on horses and all sports,' said Wiltshire, who says he has made 'a sizeable investment' on the project. 'I decided to go into this because my racecourse business has been seriously affected by the betting exchanges and I think this is the way forward.

'A lot of the old-time bookmakers who have sold their pitches and left the game now enjoy betting at home on their computers, where there are no expenses. Although the betting ring is still very strong, you now find the Betfair prices are the first show at the races, and I have been using Betfair as a hedging facility.

'I think Betfair is a marvellous service and it is the old adage – if you can't beat them, join them.'

Wiltshire is looking to cater for ordinary punters, not high-rollers, and believes using his name on the site will instil confidence in the business. He went on: 'Exchange betting is the future of gambling and although I will still be on the racecourse at the big meetings, on other days I won't be there as much as I have been in the past.'

I had long been aware that the nature of betting on the racecourse was changing. For one thing, the good old days of recording a wager through those colourful betting tickets and simply entering it in the ledger had given way to the computer age.

The punter still asked the bookie for the bet and handed over the money, but instead of one of those lovely old tickets would be given, as a receipt, a little slip on which the computer had printed the stake, the odds, and the return in the unlikely event of the horse winning.

The old ticket was simply a reference to the bet number that had been entered in the ledger and did not itself record the exact details of the bet – although most punters would make a note on the reverse as soon as they had the ticket.

With computerised betting slips there was less chance of a dispute arising because of some lack of clarity in the communication between bookmaker and punter, but somehow – and it was punters as well as bookmakers who felt this – a great deal of the charm and informality, the trust even, seemed to go out of the betting transaction once computers were introduced.

It wasn't only with regard to the tickets. The new betting-ring technology meant an end to the decades-long era of bookmakers chalking up the prices – literally, with a piece of chalk – on the board. Now the odds appeared all neatly on the computer screen. Punters soon got used to the new method – they had no choice – but many still hankered for the old.

But a much greater revolution in the world of betting was brought about by the arrival of betting exchanges – notably Betfair, which was far and away the market leader. Hence my considered opinion that if you can't beat them, join them.

When I set up www.garywiltshire.com early in 2002, Betfair was less than three years old but had already put itself in the position of the leading betting exchange by a very long way.

In terms of betting practice, the principle of an exchange is simple enough. It allows punters to bet at odds set by other punters rather than at odds set by the traditional bookmakers. They can back a horse – although exchanges bet in all sorts of activities in addition to racing – to win, or, if they think it will lose, can lay it to other punters who think it will win. In that way the traditional bookmaker becomes redundant. A commission is charged on winning bets.

The most controversial aspect of the exchanges is that the facility to lay a horse potentially invites corruption, in that if a close connection of a runner knows it will not win – perhaps because of its condition, or because the jockey has been instructed to make sure it loses – they can make a profit from laying the horse, and thus the integrity of horse racing can be compromised.

The argument over whether betting exchanges have damaged that integrity has been raging almost since they were first devised, but on one aspect there is no argument whatsoever: their existence has radically altered the nature of racecourse betting.

For one thing, bookmakers can now hedge their liabilities through Betfair rather than through other on-course layers, meaning that there is less money circulating round the ring.

For another, the exchanges provide a serious alternative to the traditional bookies, and many big punters spend much of their time betting online rather than through the bookies.

Had betting exchanges been around on Dettori Day, there is no way that Fujiyama Crest would have gone off at 2-1. Any exchange punter with half a brain would have been offering to lay Frankie's seventh ride and the likelihood is that Fujiyama Crest would have been sent off at around 8-1.

As I said in that *Racing Post* story, exchanges are the future of betting and, whether we like it or not, we have to get used to the change they've brought about.

I've never been one to resist new technology for the sake of it and on the launch day of my exchange, 1 March 2002, the *Racing Post* published my answers to questions about my own online life:

How much do you use the internet?

Mostly pre-racing and then in the evening after I come back. All the divorce lawyers love the internet. I get all the earache going from my wife Sue. It causes more rows than anything else, having the internet at home – in one million houses it's the same. If I had the choice of going to the cinema or playing on the internet, I'd play on the internet.

Which are your favourite sites?

Anything to do with sport. I use Betfair.com quite a lot and PGAtour.com to follow the major golf scores round by round. Live [in-game] football betting for me is unbelievable . . .

What do you like about using the internet?

It has taken over. A year ago I would not have known how to use a computer, even how to turn it on. Since we've had to use one under the new rules at the track, that's given me a start.

What I like is that the days of getting bluffed by book-makers saying, 'I'm full on that horse, I can't lay that', are gone. The money is there on the betting exchanges.

I've got a name as a racecourse bookmaker and some-times my local betting shops won't take my bets. Behind the button no one knows who you are.

As a bookmaker, what has been your response to the one-to-one sites?

I've had to join them. I've always enjoyed being a book-maker, but my business has been affected. I work off Betfair at the racecourse and use it to hedge bets taken at the track. You can't hedge in the same way at the track as the prices on the betting exchanges are bigger. The value is unbelievable.

As far as my own exchange was concerned, things did not work out well. In a market where Betfair is so hugely dominant it was difficult to attract subscribers, and we found it a struggle to keep up with the huge advertising costs. So sadly we decided to call it a day after only a few months, and Betfair took over our customers. I have this lingering feeling, however, that if we'd gone in with Dermot Desmond and Betdaq, we'd have become a serious competitor to Betfair.

But there was still money to be made at racecourses and dog tracks, and I never lost my love of betting at point-to-points – although I can remember one occasion I'd rather forget.

Sue had been clerking for me for years, ever since she'd been thrown in at the deep end at Oxford dogs. She was a very good clerk indeed – although I admit it can be difficult working with your spouse, and every now and again we didn't quite see eye to eye.

We were making a book at the Heythrop, near Chipping Norton in Oxfordshire – one of the most upmarket fixtures in the point-to-point calendar – and I'd got well stuck into getting one favourite beat.

The runners were on the first circuit and I was watching the race through my binoculars, when Sue came up and grabbed my arm to get my attention – and then she started going on about how some other bookmaker had come up and demanded a bet, as I hadn't wiped the chalk off our board and the prices were still up there.

I pushed her away ever so gently and said I had to watch the race, and I suppose I might just have said something mild to the effect that while the race was on I was under a bit of pressure and I couldn't be bothered to sort all that out – and the next thing I knew I was watching the runners go out on their second circuit, when out of the corner of my eye I saw Sue striding off in the same direction, straight towards the road from Chipping Norton to Banbury.

She'd got the hump, and got it big!

I didn't know which to watch: the race, where I'm about to lose £1,200, or my wife striding off across the fields towards the road. Ever the professional, having started watching the race I figured out that I'd better finish, and it ended up a losing double all round: the horse I'd taken on had won and the aggrieved missus had disappeared off the radar.

When I got back later that day she was still put out, but so tired from her own epic journey – she'd gone to the nearby Little Chef and hitched a ride into Banbury, where she found the bus to take her home – that we soon made up.

This was not our first case of marital discord on the racecourse, and now I've learned to keep a close hold on both our passports, so that she can't go storming off somewhere exotic while I'm otherwise engaged.

It was nothing to do with incidents like that, but I was getting a bit stale and jaded, a bit frustrated with the bookmaking game. The coming of betting exchanges was having more and more of an effect on racecourse betting and, for me at least, the ring was losing a lot of the buzz which had made being a course bookmaker such an exhilarating experience. I was beginning to think of looking for a way out.

One day early in 2003 I was making a book on the rails at a fairly ordinary meeting at Towcester, when who should come up but Joe Scanlon, who was a very big cheese at the Tote.

'What's the game like at the moment, Gal?' he asked, all casual.

'Terrible, Joe,' I replied, 'just terrible. It's getting harder and harder to make a living. I think the game's gone – completely gone.'

'Well that's a great shame,' said Joe with a funny sort of smile, 'as I was planning to talk with you about the Tote buying all your pitches.'

8

'I'll blow her back up when I get home'

You could have knocked me down with a feather: the Tote wanted to buy my pitches. I was on the point of sinking to my knees and begging Joe Scanlon to forget what I'd just said about the game being finished, when he suggested: 'Draw me up a list of where your pitches are and what you think they're worth, and send it to me.'

It didn't take me long to do that and a short while I later drove up the Tote headquarters in Wigan to discuss the deal. They ended up buying all my racecourse pitches, nearly fifty round the country. Over the years since then I've kept a close eye on the value of those pitches and, as you'd expect, some have gone up and some have gone down. Circumstances change the value and I took particular notice of the one in the County Stand at Aintree. I sold this to the Tote for a bit over £1,000, as back then it was the first reserve rather than a guaranteed position, but when provision was made for more pitches at Aintree it came into play and is probably now worth £150,000. On the other hand, some will have come down in value, so I'm not complaining. It's a simple case of swings and roundabouts.

In addition to buying the pitches, the Tote wanted me to run the rails betting for six months or so, during which I would teach the business to Pam Sharman, who for years had been a senior member of the on-course Tote Credit team and was now switching to the rails operation. Joe wanted me to show her the ropes, and as part of the deal offered to take on my son Nicky to clerk.

I loved all my dealings with the Tote.

One year we were betting at Glorious Goodwood and Pam had to go up to Newmarket for the Friday evening and Saturday racing, leaving me to bet on the rails on my own.

The Saturday programme at Glorious Goodwood includes one of the biggest betting races of the year, the Stewards' Cup, and I persuaded Peter Jones, then Chairman of the Tote, to come and share the fun by taking the chalks for that race. There was a very hot favourite in the form of Zidane and we were laying this jolly for all we were worth – so much so that John McCririck on Channel 4 Racing was getting more and more agitated, saying that if the favourite won the Tote would be wiped out – and Peter, flourishing the chalk like an orchestra conductor with his baton, declared dramatically, 'That price is not coming off!'

But what neither Big Mac nor anyone else knew was that early on I'd gone round the ring backing Zidane at reasonable prices, so in reality on the pitch we were only hedging our bets.

As soon as the race was over Peter had to hurry off to fulfil some commitment and I started paying out to the queue of happy punters, which must have stretched as far as Selsey Bill.

While I was counting out the readies I got a phone call. It was Joe Scanlon and he sounded very agitated indeed.

'What's going on down there? Have you gone mad? What the hell have you been doing?'

It must have looked to Joe as if we'd done a million by laying the favourite at too big a price, whereas the truth was that because we'd backed Zidane early doors we had a very good book on the race. We'd only lost about £1,500 – but what with all Big Mac's ranting and raving, it was the best £1,500 you could ever get in terms of publicity.

But my worst day working the pitch for the Tote was certainly the year I was at York for the John Smith's Cup one Saturday in mid-July. This is a fixture that attracts huge crowds, many of them intent on consuming as much of the sponsor's product as they possibly can, and it's always bedlam.

We were betting on the rails, and that day it was down to me to clear everything up after racing. As I was doing so a serious booze-fuelled brawl broke out in the Tattersalls enclosure, not at all far from our pitch, and I decided to get out of there double quick. I grabbed everything within sight and made my way to the car.

It took me two hours just to get out of the car park and it was seriously late by the time I got home. We'd had a small winning day and there was money to be put in the safe – and when I'd done that I settled down to a very large gin and tonic.

On the Monday we were betting at one of those great Windsor evening meetings and, when on arrival at the racecourse

I went to get out the cash float with which we always start the racing, I realised there was £9,000 missing.

Nine grand gone – how come?

The bag had been in the safe at home and had not been touched by me or anyone else, so where was the money? Then it dawned on me that we'd left some money in the zipped-up compartment hidden in the rails pitch, and in the chaos of trying to get away with our noses intact we had probably left it behind. With any luck it would still be there.

At 6am the following morning I drove up to York from home and as soon as they let me in I went to our stand, right at the end of the rails pitches. I unzipped the little compartment and there was ... a solitary twenty-pound note! Somebody had half-inched the nine grand – and the cheeky bastard had left a score in there as a thankyou, so that I could drown my sorrows in a plate of fish and chips.

As chance would have it, one of the very best fish and chip shops on the racing circuit – called White's – was very close to York racecourse, so I went and cashed in the £20 in exchange for a large plate of plaice and chips with some mushy peas on the side, while I worked out what to do.

I went back to the racecourse and asked the security people there to look through the closed-circuit camera footage, but that drew a blank. So the only thing for it was to drive straight across the Pennines to the Tote headquarters in Wigan and come clean with them about what had happened.

I told them that rather than go through all the palaver of

filing a formal report, and have an inquiry drag on for weeks, I'd simply give them the nine grand there and then and draw a line under the episode. So that's what I did.

But if whoever nicked the nine grand happens to be reading these words, I'll say this to them: Leaving that twenty quid for fish and chips was adding insult to injury!

It was through the Tote that I got involved in going to make a book at Doncaster – not on the St Leger, but on fishing. Yes, that's right: fishing . . .

Now I've bet on all sorts of events over my life, but to be asked to make a book on the Fish 'O' Mania competition was a first – and it was a job I hadn't been angling for!

I learned to my surprise that this contest has been going on for years and years, and is very keenly fought out by anglers. There are qualifying rounds and all that sort of thing, but beyond that please don't ask me to explain the rules.

So I was coming at this sport from a position of complete ignorance, but I have my contacts in all sorts of areas of human activity – it's not what you know, it's who you know – and I gave a drink to a bloke I knew to be well informed in matters of the rod and line. He prepared a tissue – a list of the prices at which a bookmaker should start betting – for me and I soon found out that the fishing boys (and a few girls) liked nothing better than to back up their skills with the rod with a little bet – and I didn't even have to offer them bait!

One of the thickest bets I took was from the former Tottenham Hotspur footballer Mark Jones, who turned out to be an exceptionally good as well as mad-keen fisherman. I laid him ten monkeys – £500 at 10-1 – and he duly won the competition. He was so over the moon that he jumped into the lake and had to spend an age drying out his betting slips before he came to collect.

And one more thing about Fish 'O' Mania: betting each-way there was strictly Win and Plaice!

Another new experience brought about by being with the Tote was when I became the first bookmaker to make a book at the Burghley Horse Trials. My inside knowledge of three-day eventing is about as profound as my knowledge of fishing, so again I found the right contact – this time a very refined equestrian celebrity – and crossed his palm with silver in return for the tissue, and then I was away.

The dressage was on the first day and the cross-country on the second, and on the morning of the third day one of the complete outsiders – or at least a complete outsider according to my toff's tissue – was still just about in the hunt.

But according to my expert this horse had no chance whatsoever of winning the whole competition, so I priced it up at 100-1, and as the show jumping was about to start had stood this horse for around £100,000.

It was part of the routine to ring the Tote's head office at intervals and report on the day's business.

'Have we got any liabilities today, Gary?' was the standard question, and when from Burghley I said I was standing one for £100,000 they nearly fainted in horror.

The horse didn't win, but yet again I'd stuck my neck out. One day I'll learn . . .

The MC at Fish 'O' Mania had been my old mate John McDonald and when one year the Tote was asked to be the official bookmaker at one of the big darts competitions, the Players Championship at the Circus Tavern, near Purfleet in Essex, I was asked to go along and do the odds.

John had the idea that before the Saturday evening session I should do a short spiel about the odds for the upcoming matches and, since nothing about the world of professional darts is understated, that I should make a grand entrance. There were these large red curtains through which the players ceremonially emerged before each game, and John's idea was for me to come out of those.

The final session that Saturday was due to start at 7.30pm and most of the fans had been putting pints away since about noon, so by the time I was due to make my appearance the atmosphere, while very good-natured, was extremely rowdy.

I stood behind the curtains waiting for John to introduce me, and after he'd called in vain for a little hush he announced: 'Ladies and gentlemen – you all like a bet. Well, remember the horse that won last year's Derby? We are privileged to have with us this evening the very man who rode that Derby winner – his jockey!' The curtains parted and out strode not a Derby-winning jockey but yours truly.

And as if with one voice, the thousands packed into the Circus Tavern that evening started chanting:

YOU FAT BASTARD!
YOU FAT BASTARD!
YOU FAT BASTARD!
YOU FAT BASTARD!

It got louder and louder and louder, and I never was able to make myself properly heard over the din. The things I do to earn a living!

That chanting was all in fun, but another darts event had a really nasty side to it.

I'd gone to Ireland to bet at a darts competition at the City West, a huge hotel just off the road from Dublin to Naas. SkyBet was sponsoring the competition and told me I'd be welcome to make a book there if I liked, so I asked my Irish mate Shane Rooney to join me.

As is so often the case at darts contests, the mood was very rowdy and boisterous, and when running the book it was quite a struggle for us to keep everything under control, so we had a helper in the shape of Sue's son Liam.

One game featured a little-known Irish fellow against the great Phil 'The Power' Taylor, who is such a brilliant darts player that he was runner-up to A.P. McCoy in the 2010 BBC Sports Personality of the Year. This was clearly no contest and we priced The Power at a prohibitive 1-16.

After Phil had won a young lad came to our pitch to be paid out. He'd had a bet doubling up the winner of an earlier game at even money and The Power at . . . 6-1. Somehow in the bedlam

Liam had mistakenly put 6-1 on this fellow's slip rather than 1-16, and there's quite a difference!

I pointed out the 1-16 on our board and tried to persuade the punter that it had been an obvious mistake. But he was having none of it and insisted on being paid out at the odds on the slip. After a while I realised I was getting nowhere and agreed to pay him out, at which point a great gang of his mates who had made the same bet came over. Poor Liam had put 6-1 on all their slips – I don't think he'll want to be a bookie after that experience – and we were forced to pay them all or risk the evening turning into a full-scale riot.

As soon as we'd done so we packed up the pitch – although there was another round of the competition to go – and made straight for the ferry, vowing never to get ourselves into the position of facing thirty irate punters with the drink on them.

And by the way: we still broke level on the night!

You might just have noticed in these pages the odd mention of food: the bacon sandwiches cooked for my classmates, the seafood, the carveries, the occasional helping of fish and chips, etc. etc.

And it will not surprise you to learn that as I got older that enthusiasm for food started to show itself in my waistline. The more my girth expanded, the more I seemed to want to eat, and try as I might – yes, I'm a regular at Weight Watchers in Redditch every Tuesday – I just couldn't bring my physique back to anything like the shape I was when I played in goal for Islington Schoolboys.

The heaviest I've ever reached was over 32 stone – that's about four Kieren Fallons – but my waistline has seemed to become part of my personality. And since there was no point in pretending that it wasn't there I tried to turn it to my advantage: after all, I could hardly object to being dubbed 'larger than life' in practically every article ever written about me, and being that size at least did make me instantly recognisable.

Sometimes the problems that being this large caused me were almost comic. One year we were on holiday in Lanzarote and after breakfast I made my way to the side of the hotel swimming pool to get a good draw for the day. I spied an unoccupied sun-lounger and went to grab it. I was just stretching myself out on it when part of the supporting frame suddenly snapped in half and I was unceremoniously dumped on the floor. Everybody was looking – some in sympathy but many more in scarcely controllable mirth – but no one came to help me, and all I could do was lie there and get my breath back. When I eventually managed to haul myself to my feet and walk gingerly back to my room, I noticed that the backs of both my legs had been badly cut.

But my weight occasionally got me into far worse trouble than that. In August 2003, this story appeared in the *Racing Post*, complete with the mandatory outing of 'larger than life' in the first sentence:

> *Bookmaker Gary Wiltshire will not be quite the same larger-than-life figure when he returns to racecourse duty later*

this week, having been ordered by doctors to shed seven stone in weight.

The warning follows the admission to hospital of one of Britain's best-known on-course bookmakers for the second time this year.

Wiltshire has been found to be suffering from cellulitis, a bacterial infection of the skin and tissue which, in his case, flares into fever.

The order to slim down has forced Wiltshire to reassess a diet that has consisted largely of fast food.

'At Christmas, McDonald's don't send me a card, they send me a leather briefcase because I'm one of their best customers,' said Wiltshire, who blames his eating habits on the travelling involved driving 80,000 miles a year to and from racetracks and greyhound meetings.

He was taken ill again on Wednesday and weighed in at 28st 10lb when taken into hospital.

'I have been told to lose 7st, which scares me to death, but I have lost 1st 4lb after only being in here for a few days,' said Wiltshire, who expects to be released on Tuesday.

He went on: 'I have now had a couple of warnings and I don't want a third. I will definitely be taking things a lot easier in future. It is no good dashing around the country and grabbing something to eat at fast-food joints when I get the chance the way I have been doing.

'This problem I have had makes you really hot and you get a fever with it.'

Wiltshire added: 'Other than my weight, I am healthy, and after this I guarantee that the next time I am seen on the racecourse I am going to be thinner.'

I was out of hospital within a few days as I'd expected but can't guarantee that I lost the desired seven stone.

It's all very well making jokes out of the issue of weight – like when I wrote a *Daily Mirror* column in which I was billed as 'The Belly from the Telly' – but I'm well aware that over the years my weight has been slowly killing me, and that's a pretty horrible thing to have to admit.

I've told myself that if I could get down to around 25st then at least I could walk around normally, rather than huff and puff and wheeze like I do now.

Sometimes I wonder how much my weight is down to eating while travelling and how much it's really down to the mindset of a gambler like me. By which I mean: if you've had a bad day, you want to take it out on someone, so you stop at the garage on the way home for a bar of chocolate, or you get a hamburger at McDonald's or a slab of fish and a bag of chips or a Chinese takeaway.

And that sort of gambling life means that as often as not you eat at the wrong time of day, which simply makes matters worse.

But there is hope on the horizon. The doctors at the Parkway Private Hospital have recommended that I have fitted a gastric band, which reduces the opening of the stomach and forces you to eat less. It's worth a try – but the trouble is, the first appointment they made for me was for the day before the Cheltenham Festival, and I was down to do a preview, so had to cancel the appointment …

In October 2003 I started making a book at the greyhound track at Sittingbourne, between Gillingham and Faversham in Kent.

Sittingbourne dogs had a character all its own, especially during the holiday season, when East Enders would come down and stay in caravans and chalets on the nearby coast. And by then – mainly thanks to Dettori Day – I had a good profile, so the track were very pleased to have me there.

After a while I stopped betting at Sittingbourne as the travelling was getting too much and I had too many other commitments, but in 2009 I agreed to go back there. The track had lost its contract with BAGS – the Bookmakers' Afternoon Greyhound Service, which transmitted live pictures into betting shops – because, as the *Racing Post* put it, there had been 'a suggestion of a loss of confidence in the betting market.' Betting shops were therefore hesitant about taking bets on the action at the track, and without the BAGS contract there was a serious funding problem.

So when the manager Roger Cearns approached me and asked me to return, I felt I owed it to the sport to show willing. Greyhound racing had been very good to me over the years and I wanted to help the track back on to its feet.

And a bonus was that it meant coming into close contact again with some of the great of the place, like the great bookmaker Curly Wilson, alongside whom I'd bet in the old days

185

at places like Ramsgate, while my clerk was 'Lofty', my driver Steve Cook. For the last few years Lofty has been a major presence in my life – always at the end of the phone if I needed his help and always ready with a lovely lobster to cheer me up when I was in hospital. A real good pal.

As is my old mucker Alan Ballard, whom I first met when I was betting at Poole dogs, and to whom I talk every day about some aspect of the crazy bookmaking life.

Sittingbourne was fun, but my main work was still with the Tote – even though the original commitment was only for six months – and in June 2004, a few days before the beginning of Royal Ascot, the *Racing Post*'s Howard Wright broke some interesting news:

> *Tote punters will be able to bet on the rails for the first time since 1980 when Royal Ascot opens on Tuesday and the man on the stand will be Gary Wiltshire, who last worked at the course – but failed to register a bet – twenty-four hours after he suffered a multi-million-pound loss on Dettori Day in 1996.*
>
> *The Tote have bought Wiltshire's mix of rails and Tattersalls pitches on forty-six tracks and this week they added rails positions at Royal Ascot and on Newmarket's Rowley Mile course in a private sale. All the pitches will operate under the Totesport banner.*
>
> *Wiltshire has become a Totesport employee and will also act as an on-course media officer. He will have pitch No.15*

next Tuesday, as the Tote return to the ring with fixed-odds betting.

For Totesport managing director Joe Scanlon, the move realises a long-held ambition and completes a full house of platforms for his bookmaking division.

He said: 'This gives our customers another way in which to bet with us and will give us another valuable presence on the racecourse. Gary's larger-than-life presence alone should attract the customers, because everybody knows him, but at the same time he knows the business and I'm delighted he's working for us.'

Wiltshire added: 'I'm very excited. I'm impressed by the new branding of Totesport and this is a great new challenge, not only for me but also for the Tote.'

And on the morning of the second day of the royal meeting itself, David Ashforth wrote in the Post:

The happiest man in a packed betting ring at Royal Ascot yesterday was Gary Wiltshire.

One of gambling's great characters, Wiltshire was making his debut as the Totesport representative on the rails.

It was the Tote's first venture into rails betting since 1980 and Wiltshire's first outing as a bookmaker at Ascot since being hit for seven by Frankie Dettori in September 1996.

A delighted and relieved Wiltshire said: 'It has been very good and I'm loving it.

'To begin with I was nervous, which will surprise people, but the last time I was here was for Frankie's Magnificent Seven and, although it's a different kind of pressure to running your own business, there is still pressure.

'It's gone really well. We have been very busy for a first day, with some good account customers betting with us.'

'It's gone really well' was something of an understatement. We'd won £45,000 that day.

And the week after the royal meeting, Howard Wright wrote of my return to the rails at Ascot that 'the old adage that you can't keep a good man down seems to be working'.

What neither Howard nor David picked up, though, was the reason why for me the Tuesday of Royal Ascot 2004 would have an extra-special place in my memory.

It was the day my wife stole my car.

Sue had dressed up in her Royal Ascot finery and had come with me in the expectation of having a really good time, but I hadn't told her just how much I'd have to work that day – and after several attempts to get me to leave the pitch to Pam while Mr and Mrs Wiltshire went off and shared a nice cool bottle of champagne and some smoked salmon on brown bread, Sue finally snapped.

She disappeared and, although over the last two races I was wondering where she'd got to, it wasn't until I reached the car park after racing and saw an empty space where my Merc had been that I twigged what had happened.

Just like at the Heythrop point-to-point, Sue had taken umbrage big time – only this time she'd stolen my car and driven off, leaving her doting husband stranded.

Standing there like a lemon in the car park, I couldn't work out what to do, so I phoned Sue's mobile.

'Where are you?'

'I'm here,' she said helpfully.

'Where's "here"?'

'Here. Home.' Sue was a great one for the monosyllables that evening.

She was back in Hollywood, where she'd driven double quick, and wasn't proposing to come back and collect me.

I cadged a lift off someone as far as Bicester and there found a taxi to take me to Hollywood – where I made my peace with Sue, retrieved my car, and then drove all the way back to the Ascot area, where I somehow managed to find a room in the Hilton Hotel in Bracknell. Talk about going the long way round!

That 2004 meeting was the last Royal Ascot before the stands on the Berkshire racecourse, most of which dated back only to the 1960s, were knocked down and replaced with a spanking new stand, which opened in 2006. When the 'old' grandstand was being cleared out prior to the demolition boys coming in, the course held an auction of some of the Ascot equipment at Sotheby's office in Olympia.

One of the great glories of the old course had been the number board on the inside of the track, where all the basic information – such as jockeys, going, results and starting prices – was displayed for racegoers, and some of the items being flogged off for charity were the signs from that board, including the one that read '7th Race'.

I'd tried to buy the board that read 'L. Dettori', but it went for £550, which was a bit beyond my budget. But I did manage to secure the '7th RACE' board for only seventy quid – a proper souvenir of an unforgettable occasion.

The profile I'd had from having done a million on Dettori was getting even higher through working for the Tote, and I was asked to work for Sky Sports as – along with the genial Dave Smith – their man in the betting ring at dog tracks.

This has proved to be a dream job, not least because of the banter Dave and I keep up throughout the coverage. I remember at the top of one show Dave asking me how things were going and I was able to reply: 'To be honest, Dave, it's not been a great day. I let the girlfriend down badly this morning – still, I'll blow her back up when I get home.' Boom, boom! – but I very nearly got the sack over that. Apparently it was far too racy for our refined viewing audience.

Working for Sky is always great *craic* – not only with Dave but with all the rest of the crew as well, and in particular commentator Errol Bligh, Jeff Stelling, the front man when I joined up, and good old Gary Newbon, a professional to his fingertips.

I first met Gary at the dogs at Hall Green in Birmingham. He wasn't working for Sky that night but came up and introduced himself. Of course, I'd been watching him for years covering football and boxing, and he was a legend in the Midlands sporting scene. But I pretended that I didn't know who he was, and innocently asked, 'Are you a cameraman then?' He roared with laughter, and ever since we've been the very best of friends as well as Sky colleagues who like nothing better than bouncing jokes off each other.

And I'd always lay it on a bit thick for the viewers when I really fancied a dog, as I know they'll be at home thinking, 'I hope the fat bastard gets it wrong!'

Talking of the Fat Bastard, I wonder what *Racing Post* readers made of this little piece in the paper in April 2007:

Sky Sports' betting guru Gary Wiltshire is to take part in the Flora London Marathon on Sunday 22 April and is hoping to hear from people interested in sponsoring him.

Wiltshire has been in hard training for the gruelling 26 miles and is confident of a good display. 'I've read the training manuals and the list of what to do and not to do, and would say I'm pretty well prepared,' he explained.

'I also read that Hills' Ben Clarke has lost a couple of stone as he's training for various half marathons, but I don't like halving anybody so it's the full whack for me and should do me the power of good.

'I've tried to formulate a plan for the whole route so I conserve my energy. With it being a Sunday, I can get an off-peak travelcard first thing in the morning, hop on the tube at Greenwich and hope to be in St James's Park well before lunch.

'Mind you, the bloody runners could easily get in the way of any buses I have to take.'

I only hope they noticed the date on that day's paper: 1 April.

Earlier that year had come what looked like a huge opportunity: appearing alongside Chris Tarrant of *Who Wants to be a Millionaire?* fame in a new television game called *The Colour of Money*.

The studio contained twenty cash machines, each of which had a different coloured screen, and each was loaded with a different amount of cash – anything from £1,000 to £20,000 – but the contestants, studio audience and viewers at home were not made aware of how much money was in each machine. The contestants had to accumulate a target sum of money, which required very nimble thinking on your feet, and my role was to direct the contestants to where the money was, what they should be doing to maximise their chances, and so on. The letter of agreement I was sent by the production company defined my part as 'a game advisor in the pilot where you will provide your expert advice on, without limitation, game strategy and statistics to the contestants (for the avoidance of doubt, such contestants shall be free to accept, follow or ignore such advices at their sole discretion).'

I went up to London to meet Chris and talk about the game, and we got on really well. Recording the pilot programme took three days, and I was put up in Jury's Hotel in Welbeck Street and collected every morning by a chauffeur-driven car. For once in my life I was being treated like a film star, but it didn't last long. ITV1, which was broadcasting *The Colour of Money*, presumably decided that they needed somebody a bit more comely than The Belly from the Telly as Chris Tarrant's sidekick in the show, and I was replaced by Millie Clode.

The Colour of Money first aired in February 2009 and it got quite a hammering from some of the critics and poor viewing figures.

I watched it with very mixed feelings. Chris had been charming and there had been a real chemistry between us which I'm sure would have made the show a success – but I would say that, wouldn't I?

After I'd been ditched he sent me a letter in which he wrote: 'I was really sorry that you didn't get the show because you and I got on really well and I think it would have been great.'

But to be jocked off by a pretty girl – oh, the shame of it!

It was swings and roundabouts time again, for by the time *The Colour of Money* was axed in April 2009 after just seven episodes had been transmitted I had another string to my bow, and a very good one indeed.

Towards the end of 2008 I was approached by the BBC about making the occasional appearance on their racing coverage, and of course I leapt at the chance. Angus Loughran had been let go as the racing team's man in the betting ring following his well-publicised financial problems and, while the original booking was just for the Welsh National at Chepstow at the end of December, if all went well there were obvious possibilities of a more regular role.

All seemed to go well enough – at least according to John

McCririck, my main opposition on Channel 4 Racing, in his newspaper column in the first week of January 2009:

Drafting ebullient racecourse bookie Gary Wiltshire into the BBC team at Chepstow last Saturday was inspired.

With much missed Angus Loughran departing after eight years their coverage of the Ladbroke at Ascot last month proved somewhat threadbare.

Statto had been one of more than a dozen betting-ring reporters tried by the Beeb going back to the late bon viveur and punter Charles Benson twenty-five years ago.

All had brought their individual, idiosyncratic approach to interpreting the nuances of the jungle but none could possibly have the insight, or depth of girth, of Wiltshire.

Famously he went skint over Frankie Dettori's Magnificent Seven at Ascot.

Being a decent gentleman he sold his house so that everyone got paid and, after re-establishing his horse and greyhound course business, Totesport snapped him up for their rails pitches.

A regular standby for a quick word on Channel 4, his Large and Large gambling-savvy banter with the ubiquitous Dave Smith from greyhound track rings is a cult highlight of Sky's all-embracing dog coverage, usually on Tuesday evenings.

Watching a recording of Chepstow, steered expertly as usual by the ravishing Clare Balding, I was at the disadvantage of knowing the outcome.

But Wiltshire's twinkly-eyed humour and practical-
ly Byzantine knowledge of what his mockers were up to
added enormously to the programme . . .

I'd love to see Wiltshire take on quick-witted John Par-
rott when the BBC returns to our screens at Aintree in
April. Show that marginally less fat arm-waving loud-
mouth on Channel 4 just how it should be done!

Gal appearing with John Parrott – now there was a thought …

I must have been doing something right at the Welsh National, as I was booked for more BBC television work and my first official day as the Beeb's man in the betting ring came at Ascot – so many of my ups and downs have been there – on St Valentine's Day 2009.

Then I got a call from Dermot Cumiskey, editor of the BBC racing coverage. He'd liked how I'd done at Chepstow and Ascot and now wanted me – just as Big Mac had suggested – to pair up with John Parrott and do a sort of betting-ring double act on the biggest racing occasions.

I wasn't so sure.

I'd known John a good while, a bit through his time as a top-rate snooker player but much more through seeing him at the races. In fact, I was such a fan of his that when years ago the *Sporting Life* asked me for its 'Lifestyles' column to name my sporting hero outside racing, I said: 'John Parrott, the snooker star who has never forgotten his roots and loves a day at the races.'

And that was long, long before I knew I could be working with John.

No, I had no problem whatsoever with John himself. My hesitation was on account of whether the idea of bringing together a chirpy Cockney like me and a down-to-earth Scouser like John would work.

Dermot tried to reassure me on that score. 'If you'll just be yourselves,' he said, 'it'll be like two mates talking in the pub about the racing and the betting.'

And he was right.

I had to clear my new BBC role with Sky – who were well chuffed, as the new job raised my profile but didn't clash directly with their greyhound coverage – and I had to pack in working on the Tote racecourse pitches, where on televised days there could clearly be the sort of conflict of interests about which the Beeb is very sensitive. I appreciated that I was taking a gamble with regard to my working life and that my new profile would sometimes cause problems when I went into a betting shop in search of a decent wager, but joining the BBC racing team was a no-brainer.

That February day at Ascot was fairly quiet, but the next racing fixture on the BBC schedule was the very biggest: the 2009 Grand National. When we were going through the betting I was very dismissive of the chances of the complete outsiders – 'They've got four legs, and that's about all you say can about them' – and the 100-1 shots included Mon Mome, who went on and won the great race fair and square.

A while later I was at Chepstow when this sweet lady came up and said: 'Aren't you that person who said my horse had four legs but had no chance?'

I had no idea who she was, and was giving her the 'Hello, love, how's your day going?' patter when she interrupted me and said that she was Mrs Bingham, who owned Mon Mome. I told her I was ever so sorry and had nearly got the sack – one of my standard defences! – over those comments, and she replied, 'You'll learn one day.' But I don't think I ever will.

And then came the Flat season, when the first big BBC coverage was the Derby meeting at Epsom Downs, with Clare Balding joined by the irrepressible former champion jockey Willie Carson.

Derby Day is the only day outside Royal Ascot when the dress code in the posh enclosure is morning suit, and all BBC presenters are expected to turn up in the required outfit.

Diana Keen, one of the production managers on the BBC racing programmes, told me I'd need a morning suit for Derby Day and recommended that I hire one from the traditional supplier, Moss Bros. So I went into Birmingham one morning to pick one up.

Easier said than done, I soon discovered. At Moss Bros they were terribly helpful and dug out the largest morning coat they had, but I had more chance of swimming the English Channel with a double bed on my back than I had of squeezing my ample form into that. I suppose they didn't have too many customers with a 60-inch waist and a 68-inch chest, so had no great need to keep such a size in stock.

Trying to work out what to do, I went along to a Birmingham shop called John Banks Big and Tall Menswear (the John

Banks not to be confused with the famous bookmaker!), where the manager Ian Oliver suggested I leave everything to him and he'd get it all sorted.

He was as good as his word, contacting a tailor in India who must have had an excess of fabric and set about constructing a coat large enough to contain me.

But with all this coming and going I was cutting things a bit fine, as Derby Day was getting closer and closer. With only two days to go before the big race – and one day before Oaks day on the Friday, when there is no longer a dress code of morning wear – I had to make my way to Finsbury Square in London to collect the morning suit. There were a few amendments to be made, but by Derby Day all had been made perfect and I finished up looking a picture – and the pockets in the coat were so big that Willie Carson could easily have snuggled up in one.

After its maiden voyage on Derby Day the morning coat was put away – I never did check whether Willie was hiding in one of the pockets – for just a couple of weeks before being rolled out again for Royal Ascot.

This, of course, would be my first royal meeting for the BBC and it meant a great deal to me that all should go well. So what happened before racing on the Thursday, the third day of the meeting, came as a terrible shock.

We'd had our usual production meeting in the morning, when all issues that might affect the day's coverage were aired and the schedule carefully gone through so that everyone knew what's what. Royal Ascot is unlike any other race meeting for the BBC because there is such a strong element of fashion to be woven into the racing, so that meeting is of major importance.

But all had gone well for me on the opening two days and there were no major problems anticipated for that afternoon, so I was in a very relaxed frame of mind when, after a little light breakfast, I returned to my car to study the form and work out what in particular needed to be covered from the ring that afternoon, Gold Cup day.

The phone in my car rang. It was a mate and he didn't beat about the bush.

'Have you seen this morning's *Daily Mail*?'

'No – why?'

'Read the Charlie Sale diary.'

With no idea what all this was about, I went and borrowed a *Daily Mail* from a punter sitting in a nearby car. I turned to the sports pages and in the Charles Sale 'Sports Agenda' diary column read this:

> *BBC director-general Mark Thompson's inspection of his troops at Ascot on Tuesday included a visit to the rails to meet betting guru Gary Wiltshire. This seal of approval suggests it doesn't bother the DG that the Beeb somehow now employ as their odds pundit a former bookmaker with the Tote who went bankrupt after Frankie Dettori rode all seven winners at Ascot in 1996.*

Bankrupt?! Yes, I took a great big hammering thanks to Frankie, but I was never bankrupt. If the Beeb thought I'd been bankrupt, they'd never have kept me on for a second. Here, right in the middle of one of the biggest days of the year, my BBC career was at a crossroads.

I phoned my solicitor in London, who said that he'd do his best to get a retraction from the *Mail* before we went on air.

Those next few minutes were possibly the most nerve-wracking of my life – yes, even more than watching Fujiyama Crest come up the straight – and it really felt like my future hung in the balance.

Then, just when I was beginning to think that I'd better start making my way home, the lawyer phoned. The *Mail* had acknowledged its blunder and was offering to settle out of court. I could go ahead.

And this paragraph duly appeared in the Charles Sale column:

> *Earlier in Ascot week, I suggested that new BBC betting guru Gary Wiltshire had once 'gone bankrupt'. In fact, although Mr Wiltshire made substantial losses after Frankie Dettori rode all seven winners in one day at Ascot in 1996, he was never made bankrupt.*
>
> *I am happy to put the record straight and sincerely apologise for any embarrassment that may have been caused.*

Sorted! – and in the nick of time.

9

'There's no better pill than a winning pill'

I've seen the future of betting. It's in an office on a housing estate in Rumney, a suburb on the eastern side of Cardiff. From the outside it looks a totally unremarkable place, though you might pause to wonder why there are so many flash cars in the car park.

Since 2005 this nondescript location has been an office for players on the betting exchanges. Inside there are rows of desks on which sit computer keyboards. On the desks and around the walls are more television screens than you could shake a stick at, some of them showing the sporting action from all over the world, others on which you can monitor the ever-fluid exchanges on Betfair.

Welcome to the world of betting in the new millennium.

This set-up was founded by the late bookmaker John Lovell, the man credited with pioneering the computerisation of on-course betting and a good friend of mine who loved point-to-points as much as he loved the greyhounds.

After John was tragically killed in a road accident in 2008 the business was carried on with great success by his sons David and James, and it provides a dream venue for those who like to play on the exchanges. Indeed, it's a living monument to John's motto: 'There's no better pill than a winning pill.'

The year before John's tragic death, David Ashforth of the *Racing Post* had made his way to Rumney:

Visiting the John Lovell Betting Exchange Office near Cardiff is an eye-opening experience. On an afternoon when the sole race meeting was at Catterick, the shop was virtually full, and it was no ordinary shop.

Traditional over-the-counter betting is available, but accounts for less than two per cent of business. The shop is geared to the needs of Betfair users. There are 24 terminals, each with an adjacent screen showing SIS, or other channels. The clientele is exclusively male, but also exclusively young, most in their early twenties.

Lovell, a bookmaker who pioneered on-course computerised betting in Britain, enjoys the unfamiliar experience of hoping that his customers win a lot of money: 'Its success depends on having successful punters because the people here are not casual punters, betting for fun, they are betting to win, like City traders. I do all I can to help them win, by providing the best, fastest connections, one-click software, and the best supply of pictures.'

Lovell's son, David, has played a big part in attracting customers, and leads a mutual help system, with customers learning from each other.

Lovell snr says: 'I've learnt that you need young people.

Older people just aren't quick enough, and don't last. Young ones speak a Betfair language. It is a different era.'

The players here are very quick on the keyboard, betting largely in-running. David Lovell, backing and laying, in and out rapidly, said: 'It is more like playing a computer game than reading a race, and sometimes involves trying to capitalise on the major changes that can take place towards the end of a race.'

Collectively, the shop's customers have over half a million pounds in Betfair accounts, and some are clearly very successful. Brett Lloyd, at 36 probably the oldest in the shop, said: 'It has changed my life. I never used to bet in-running but, with SIS right next to the terminal, I have been very successful. I started last September and now have a new apartment on Cardiff Bay and a new car.'

A nineteen-year-old Cardiff University student, who asked to remain anonymous, said: 'I started almost a year ago and have won over £100,000, largely backing horses in-running. I have been taught by David Lovell – we help each other. It needs discipline and patience. Having SIS right next to the terminal is a big help.' ...

They are a friendly group of bright young men, whom Lovell charges up to £30 a day for the use of the facilities. He also has a commission-sharing agreement with Betfair ...

There is no doubt about the attractiveness of the facilities Lovell offers to exchange users, particularly having an SIS screen next to each terminal, but it remains to be seen whether it is a business model viable on a national scale …

For the big bookmakers, offering shop customers ready access to unadjusted exchange prices could simply divert business from more profitable, higher-margin SP bets.

The punters at the John Lovell Betting Exchange Office don't have to know anything about horse racing – the last time I was there I clocked only a single copy of the *Racing Post* – but instead they live on their wits, carefully watching the racing action and many of them betting purely on how well a horse is going in the race.

Those top-of-the-range cars in the car park answer any doubts about how profitable this kind of betting life can be. Many of the guys in there are regularly clearing ten grand a day, and I like the tale of one lad – a school friend of David's – who in his early twenties is one of the biggest players in the office: he's gone from stacking shelves in Asda to driving a £45,000 car and living in a mortgage-free house, and it's all down to his skill at reading a race in progress and pushing the buttons at the right time. (Mind you, his Mum likes him still to work the odd day in Asda, just to keep his feet on the ground!)

Nice work if you can get it, and anyone can get it if they're sharp enough: being on the ball is the key to making it pay. The pictures of the racing and greyhound action come through Satellite Information Services (SIS), which does not have the same time delay as the pictures the punters could watch on their computers at home. So the punters in that Cardiff office have an advantage over housebound punters who are matching their bets.

But even for those playing the exchanges from home, it's like having a betting shop in your front room – and a betting shop which never closes. With the internet and satellite or digital television you can find sporting action from somewhere round the world at any time of the day or night – and wherever there is sporting action, there is someone ready and keen to take a bet on it.

Purists might say that betting in that sort of way lacks all the spice of the traditional ways – the wheeling and dealing and the schemes, some of which you'll have read about in this book – and of course they would be right. But you only have to be aware of the astonishing commercial success of Betfair to know that there are plenty of punters who love sitting down and playing the exchanges, and make a considerable profit from it.

And as with the traditional means of betting, it's all about getting an advantage – as that Irish lad who got 6-1 against Phil 'The Power' Taylor that day in Ireland found out! – and with exchange betting every second, even every nanosecond, counts. So some players have taken to renting hospitality boxes at racecourses and playing from there, where the action will be completely live, and not subject to any time delay whatsoever.

On the other hand, old-school punters like me prefer to know, when we're making a bet, just who we might be getting into bed with. Make your wager with a bookmaker and you know who you're up against, while a bet on the exchanges could be with anyone, even – heaven forbid! – the owner or trainer.

Betting exchanges certainly make for a truer market. In the old days you went to Towcester and there were twenty bookies in the ring who made the market, and if the big firms wanted to come in and shorten one up it was fairly easy for them to do so – unless Wiltshire was taking a stand, of course!

But with the exchanges you're not talking about twenty people with an opinion, but twenty thousand – and twenty thousand people can't be wrong.

I've mentioned already how the betting scene has changed through the coming of the betting exchanges and computerisation, and one consequence of this if that there just don't seem to be so many of the great punting characters around as before.

As I've just said, I always wanted to know who I was up against when taking a decent bet, and there were several characters in Midlands racing whom I knew were especially canny, and therefore to be treated with great caution when they approached my pitch.

The legendary Dodger McCartney was loved by everybody – he was forever joking with the owners, trainers and jockeys – and a great deal of the buzz went out of the ring when he left us. But I'm not sure that his punting success quite matched up to the legend.

Then there was Johnny Hurndale, nicknamed 'Johnny Lights' because the colour of his face would switch like the colours of traffic lights when he was losing big.

Phil Jordan would only bet when he was convinced that the percentage figures were soundly in his favour. His catchphrase was always, 'Anything for the weekend, Sir?' when he came up to back a horse. Henry Gould loved having ten grand on a short-priced one: his speciality was hunter chases – but sadly, like too many others, he's no longer with us.

Charles Eden, a regular at Worcester, could bet big but always left it very late, just as the runners were coming under orders. He loved watching you sweat as you took his money just before the off and so didn't have time to offload any of it.

And a fellow we called Novice Hurdle Mick came on the scene from nowhere a few years ago and thought nothing of having seven or eight grand on a horse. He disappeared as quickly as he appeared. Wherever he is, I hope he's OK, and still putting the frighteners on the bookies.

Every day another one seems to have gone from the scene, and they're not being replaced, as so many of the big punters are now holed up somewhere staring at a computer screen.

In the old days a bookie would get a couple of favourites turned over and get back home as soon as he could for a bit of canoodling with the missus. Nowadays he's more likely to want her to rub some liniment into his neck, as it's gone all stiff from staring at a computer screen all day.

The atmosphere in the betting rings has changed, as fewer bookmakers are prepared to stick their necks out. Everybody seems to be going the same price a good deal of time, and there's an unwritten law that you can't put a price higher than Betfair's.

In the on-course market the independents are struggling to keep their end up in a market dominated by the High Street chains, especially the Big Three of Ladbrokes, William Hill and Coral, and there is no better illustration of that than how the Big Three push down on-course prices on the Grand National. In 2010 a concerted effort to push down prices meant that the over-round on the race (that is, the combined odds of the whole field in percentage terms – the higher it is, the less advantageous to the punter) was a whopping 155 per cent: in other words, bookies would in theory pay out £100 for every £155 they took in.

This story appeared in the *Racing Post* two days after the race:

BBC betting expert Gary Wiltshire, while not excusing the SP overround of 155 on the John Smith's Grand National – the worst for at least twenty years – said on Sunday that bookmakers did not have time to react in the face of what he described as the most chaotic scenes he had ever seen in the Aintree ring.

During the build-up to the race, Wiltshire highlighted that despite the number of horses being backed very few were lengthening in price, and this was reflected in a book heavily weighted against the punters.

Wiltshire said: 'I think the bookies were so busy, they just didn't have time to react to the market. I have never seen anything like it in twenty-odd years of going to the meeting.

'In the hour before the race punters were queued at least twenty deep in front of the bookmakers. At the same time, the offices were backing about a dozen of the runners.'

According to Wiltshire, the off-course firms initially attempted to shorten Big Fella Thanks before the gamble on winner Don't Push It gained momentum.

They also piled into Hello Bud, Cloudy Lane, Comply Or Die, My Will, Mon Mome, Dream Alliance, Royal Rosa, Beat The Boys, Nozic and The Package.

'As soon as we got there at midday, the offices went in to back Big Fella Thanks and shortened it to 9-1, but that didn't work, and he went off 10-1 joint-favourite. However, they were successful in shortening the other eleven horses,' said Wiltshire.

'I've bet at Aintree, and have never seen so many people trying to get on horses. Bookies, because they were doing so much business, were shortening the horses they were laying, and that was it.

'I don't know if the bookies were using exchanges or not. If they had they would have backed it back and gone bigger, but they never did. The bookies had a captive audience and did not have to offer big prices.'

He added: 'It is all right saying the winner paid more on the exchanges but don't forget Betfair's market is win-only, and on the Grand National most punters want to play each-way.'

That halving of the price of Don't Push It was almost all down to money from the offices, and the obvious moral, for regular punters as well as those once-a-year folk who like a flutter on the nation's greatest race, is: when betting on the Grand National, always take an early price rather than wait until later on. The chances of your horse going out in the market is remote.

Once a gambler, always a gambler. I've got grandchildren now and I want to spend time with them, but what with Sky and the BBC and audio work for Tote betting shops and the odd point-to-point and making a book at Sittingbourne dogs – where the BAGS contract has happily been restored – I seem to have even less time than I ever did.

It's funny how different parts of my life connect. When I was betting at Oxford dogs the trainer to keep an eye on there was John Peterson – always the man to follow when the money was down. John retired, but his son Michael has taken over, and guess what: my youngest son Charlie, who was born a few weeks after Dettori Day, has just bought a greyhound and Michael Peterson is training him.

My eldest son Nicky started clerking at the age of eighteen, and it's beginning to look as if Charlie is inclined to follow him. As I said at the very beginning of this book, that love of gambling must be in the blood.

I'm always being asked for tips on how to beat the bookies, and it was originally my intention in the last chapter of this book to give you a few. But on reflection I don't want to insult your intelligence with all that 'Betting in doubles and trebles is a mug's game' sort of spiel, or to tell you that you get nowhere without inside knowledge – whatever my own experience was with those donkeys down at Combe Haven!

Most of the daily papers nowadays carry top-class racing information, and the trade daily the *Racing Post* contains a mind-boggling amount of information which no serious punter should ignore (and I'm not saying that because Racing Post Books is the publisher of this volume). My only advice is: get as much information as you can, and filter it as intelligently as you can. Simple as that!

Despite the changes in the business which I've talked about in this book, I wouldn't put anyone off becoming a bookmaker if they're so inclined. Indeed, I've run bookmaking classes, and I'm proud that after nearly forty years in the game – more if you count that grim experience with Charlottown when I was at school! – I'm passing on some of my knowledge of the bookmaking art to others, to people who might be looking for a change of career, and win lots of money into the bargain. If you like the idea of learning more about the bookmaking life, just email me via:

www.garywiltshire.co.uk

or write to me c/o Sittingbourne dogs – at Central Park Stadium, Church Road, Eurolink, Sittingbourne, Kent ME10 3SB.

I hope you've enjoyed the book.

Be lucky!

Index

Index

Index

Index

Index